Church on the Move

A Practical Guide for Ministry in the Community

G. TRAVIS NORVELL

JUDSON PRESS
PUBLISHERS SINCE 1824
VALLEY FORGE, PA

Judson Press has made every effort to trace the ownership of all quotes. In the event of a question arising from the use of a quote, we regret any error made and will be pleased to make the necessary correction in future printings and editions of this book.

Bible quotations in this volume are from the New Revised Standard Version of the Bible, copyright © 1989 by the Division of Christian Education of the National Council of the Churches of Christ in the United States of America. Used by permission. All rights reserved. And *The Holy Bible*, King James Version.

Interior design by Beth Oberholtzer.
Cover design by Anthony Aranha.

Library of Congress Cataloging-in-Publication data

Names: Norvell, G. Travis, author.
Title: Church on the move : a practical guide for ministry in the community / G. Travis Norvell.
Description: Valley Forge, PA : Judson Press, [2022]
Identifiers: LCCN 2021038097 (print) | LCCN 2021038098 (ebook) | ISBN 9780817018320 (paperback) | ISBN 9780817082369 (epub)
Subjects: LCSH: Communities--Religious aspects--Christianity. | Neighborliness--Religious aspects--Christianity. | Witness bearing (Christianity) | Church work.
Classification: LCC BV625 .N67 2022 (print) | LCC BV625 (ebook) | DDC 253--dc23
LC record available at https://lccn.loc.gov/2021038097
LC ebook record available at https://lccn.loc.gov/2021038098

Printed in the U.S.A.

First printing, 2022.

*This book is dedicated to
Creigh Monroe "Monty" Halstead
(1971–1990)*

Contents

Acknowledgments

I would like to thank the congregation of Judson Memorial Baptist Church in Minneapolis, Minnesota, for granting me the time to write this book and the encouragement to walk, pedal, and ride the bus. I have a deep love for pastoral ministry, and Judson makes this love blossom more each day. Thanks to the Judson Press and American Baptist Home Mission Societies, especially Laura Alden, Jeffery Haggray, Michaele Birdsall, Curtis Ramsey-Lucas, Rebecca Irwin-Diehl, Gale Tull, Linda Johnson-LeBlanc, Lisa Blair, and editor Cheryl Price. Thanks also to Jay Walljaspert, Michael McGregor, Michele Molstead, Melissa Wenzel, Lou Miranda, Eric Hoeffer, Bill Lindeke, Laura Everett, William Schroeer and Pamela Fickenscher, Sara Joy Proppe, Margaret Marcuson, Laura Hartman, Jeff Sapp, Dave Walker, and Anthony Taylor, who either read parts of this book, inspired parts of it, or had conversations about the topics. I am forever indebted to the editorial work of Carol Carpenter. Furthermore, a word of gratitude to Pope Francis: I know we will never meet and even though I tried, unsuccessfully, to get you to endorse this book, I am thankful for your witness, courage, and teaching. Most of all, all my heart and thanks and gratitude to Lori, Seneca, Glen, and John for your abiding love, rolling eyes, and compassion when I say, "Let's walk instead," or "Let's go for a bike ride," or "Taking the bus would be so much more enjoyable."

Ordinary Time 2021

You've Heard It Said . . .

You've heard it said, "You have to choose between church renewal and social justice."
But I say, "You cannot have one without the other."

You've heard it said, "Small churches will be extinct by 2050."
But I say, "Small churches are exactly what the world needs at this time."

You've heard it said, "You need parking and parking lots to grow a church."
But I say, "You don't need one at all, and if you do have one, turn it into a plaza."

You've heard it said, "Only extroverted leaders can turn around an established church (and even then the odds are slim)."
But I say, "Introverts can play to their strengths to help turn around an established church."

You've heard it said, "You need an established and well-maintained social media presence to reach new people."
But I say, "They help, for sure, but what you really need is to walk, pedal, or take public transit in your neighborhood to reach your neighbors."

You've heard it said, "You need a well-trained, youthful staff to turn around a church."
But I say, "That would be great, but the staff you need is probably sitting in your pews, retired, and just waiting to be called or invited."

You've heard it said, "Churches need to rebrand themselves, change their name, and restructure their bylaws."

But I say, "Yes, those are great activities for churches to explore, but what they really need to do is explore their neighborhood, to start listening and stop talking."

Introduction

*O*ne Sunday morning in 2013, I preached a sermon asking the congregation if they would sacrifice something in their lives so that others in our community could experience more joy.[1] That evening when I went to say goodnight to my daughter, Seneca, she said, "I've been thinking about your sermon this morning. Dad, what are you willing to sacrifice so that others can have more joy?" In an instant, my mouth went ashen and I felt like a complete phony in front of my 12-year-old daughter. I did not have an answer for her. I kissed her goodnight and said, "I don't know, but we'll talk about it in the morning."

A few days earlier, the heater in my Volkswagen Passat had gone kaput. It was a terrible time for the heater to stop working. I am a pastor in Minneapolis, where winter is a six-month, teeth-chattering battle for warmth. Nevertheless, a heater-less car in a severe winter turned out to be, in the words of Elvis Costello, a brilliant mistake. For months, the idea of giving up my car had been stirring in my soul, but I could not find the courage or the imagination to make it happen. Seneca's question was the nudge I needed to make the change that had been building within me.

I stayed awake that night for hours researching car-lite options. At breakfast, I told the family I had my answer to Seneca's question. After dinner I called a family meeting to propose an experiment that would affect us all: We would neither repair the heaterless car nor buy another car. Instead, we would sell the car and I would walk, ride my bike, or take the bus to work. The look on their faces was one of horror, so I assured them this was my experiment, not theirs. And I made sure they knew we were not selling the van my wife, Lori, drives. With those assurances in hand, everyone agreed to my experiment.

I had to do something to prove to my daughter—and to myself—that I was not a phony, a hypocrite. Her question made me face the reality that I had become too comfortable, too secure in my walk with Jesus. I was tired of feeling helpless in the face of climate change, tired of being all talk and no action. I would sacrifice a small amount of convenience, choice, and comfort in order to renew my commitment to the healing of creation.

Over the course of the next couple of weeks my experiment began to take shape. I took some of the proceeds from the sale of the heater-less car and purchased metal-studded bicycle tires, a pair of heavy-duty gloves (the kind a person handling molten steel would wear), and a transit card. I reckoned that if I could make this idea work in the dead of winter, then I could easily do it year-round.

The devil on my shoulder kept questioning my decision, asking: How will you get to the nursing homes in the exurbs? How will you respond to emergencies? What will you do when it rains or snows? What about your clothes? You cannot bike in a suit. Plus, you'll arrive late and sweaty to meetings. I did not have the answers to those questions; I hoped the answers would come as I pedaled, walked, and rode the bus.

This was not my first attempt to walk, bike, or take public transit for my job as a pastor. In fact, it was my fourth-ish attempt. The dream started in divinity school, when Lori and I realized the effect our sedentary lifestyle was having on our bodies. Since we did not have the funds for a gym membership, we started walking in the evenings and biking on the weekends. Gradually, we incorporated movement into our daily activities by biking to church and walking to the grocery store or on dates. (Let it be known: Walks to the grocery store did not count as dates.) In my first parish in Athens, West Virginia, I started riding my bike around town as soon as we unpacked—until some college students threw an empty twelve-ounce brown beer bottle at me; after that I vowed never to ride my bike again.

Two years later, in Lincoln, Rhode Island, while officiating at my first funeral, I heard stories about the deceased, who did the unthinkable: He rode his bike from Lincoln to Providence year-round, every day, for forty years. The crowd smiled at the idiosyncratic memory; I smiled at the inspiration. It was enough to get me back on my bike for weekend rides, but not for my pastoral duties.

When I moved to New Orleans, I thought for sure I had found the perfect place to walk, ride, and take public transit: a flat, compact city with streetcars and no snow. Anticipating the genius of my plan, I sold my truck before we moved. After we unpacked our belongings in our new apartment in the Crescent City, I bought a bike and started pedaling. I did not anticipate, however, the daily afternoon rains (which caused small roadside lakes to appear), the effect of high humidity on a suit (I arrived at a parishioner's home one time soaked in so much sweat that he offered to get me a shirt), or the reaction of some of the congregation's leaders, who wanted me to drive rather than walk, bike, or take public transit ("Pastor, I think it's time you bought a car."). I surrendered my dream, again. I bought a VW Passat, the very car whose heater went kaput in Minneapolis.

The first few days of biking in Minneapolis were horrible. I had not ridden my bike on a regular basis in years; every inch of my body was sore afterward. Then there was the cold. In order to counter the below-zero wind that blasted through layers of clothing, I would repeat the mantra, "Mother Earth, you'd better appreciate this. Mother Earth, you'd better appreciate this."

When it rained or snowed, I took the bus. At first, I had no idea about bus routes or even how to pay for a ride. In fourteen years of ministry, I had taken the bus only once to get to the inauguration ceremonies of a newly elected mayor. I discovered that bus trips offered a course in human studies. Liberals like me may talk about diversity and economic equality, but many of us rarely spend extended time with the poor or share space with the diverse populations of the city. Riding the bus, I found myself sitting or standing beside a Somali woman reading Barbara Ehrenreich's *Nickel and Dimed*, a father of five en route from the midnight shift at McDonald's to his daytime job cleaning offices, a woman with a disability and her abusive aide, a recent college graduate on her way to a job interview, and schoolkids making their way across the city to the library. Riding in the seclusion of my car had kept me from contact or communion with all these people. I had often prayed for the welfare of my city, but I had little idea who (or what) I was praying for—until I rode the bus.

When I had a free morning or afternoon I would walk home or stroll around the neighborhood. Walking allowed me to explore local parks, smell dinners being cooked, hear the music neighbors played on their radios and with their instruments, and appreciate the wonder and complexity of the "parish." One time I threw a ball back over a fence to kids playing kickball; one time I "caught" an escaped dog that jumped into my arms after streaking down the sidewalk. Other times I would miss my bus connection and walk to my destination.

Growing up, I often heard the poor derided as lazy. As I walked the sidewalks of Minneapolis in the pouring rain or in a blizzard, like many of the working poor do, I realized they are anything but lazy.

When my pastoral destination in the exurbs was nowhere near a bus stop and too far away for a bicycle commute, parishioners offered to take me. I was uneasy with this reliance on parishioners. I did not like giving up control of the situation or surrendering my time to another driver. But many of these trips turned out to be extended pastoral visits. As on all good road trips, the discussions in the car were often deep and revealing—moments of unexpected grace.

At first, I took the new insights and imagined myself as the pastor of a bikeable parish, but then the congregation joined me, and I saw myself as the pastor of *a church on the move*. Walking, biking, taking public transit, sharing space with those with their backs against the wall, attending safe/complete streets meetings, etc. softened my heart and the hearts of the congregation, enabling us together to reimagine the promise of small city-neighborhood church ministry. If small city-neighborhood churches can embrace a church-on-the-move approach to ministry, they will find a marriage of social justice and church renewal.

Throughout the book, I use the phrase "small city-neighborhood churches." I once heard author and environmental activist Bill McKibben say, "We don't need any more corporations too big to fail. What we need are communities so small they'll succeed."[2] When I heard him say that, I felt the truth of the statement deep within my bones. It is the way forward for small church ministry. A small church is defined for this book as a church that is small enough for intimacy, small enough where you learn to love the unlovable. A small church is more than just a church where everyone knows your name; it is a church small enough where everyone knows your story.

The emphasis on city-neighborhoods or urban areas resulted from demographic shifts that we are experiencing worldwide. On May 23, 2007, based on United Nations calculations, the world shifted from majority rural to majority urban. As the world becomes more densely populated, urban and city and neighborhood ministry becomes more vital. In most American and Canadian cities, churches are already present in city centers and urban neighborhoods. We do not have to start from scratch. Rather, we have to configure how to do ministry for this time and in this place.

It took me a long time to discover this possibility. Since graduating from divinity school in 2000, I have held firmly to the idea that if a congregation just did what it does in a beautiful and authentic fashion, all would be well. By virtue of our witness, people would seek us out, which would generate new life. If the church would just commit to beautiful and authentic worship, if it offered beautiful and authentic care, education, missions, and spirituality, the rest would take care of itself. Outsiders would find us by word of mouth, people would be motivated to give, members of the community responding to the care and love in the community would devote themselves more and give more of themselves to the flourishing of the community.

In 2012 I accepted the call to be the pastor of Judson Memorial Baptist Church in Minneapolis. Judson is a small city-neighborhood church with a rich history of social activism, inclusion, the arts, talented pastors, and engaged laity. The church incarnated the ideals described above and yet despite all of its positive attributes, it was declining.

I describe Judson Church as a congregation of mostly quirky people who live at the intersection of the television shows *The Vicar of Dibley* and *Northern Exposure*. It is a church with a membership of around 150–175, averaging about 110 for worship on any given Sunday. Our most active age group is those 65 to 80, but we do have an active minority of people under 65 who work as chaplains, artists, teachers, social workers, and salespeople, along with a few engineers and doctors. Because we are in a neighborhood that is fairly stable and attractive to young families, we have about twenty-five children from cradle to twelfth grade. In the midst of the 150–175 are a baker's dozen of ordained members, plenty of members of the fraternities/sororities "Phi Kappa" and "Mu Kappa" (Preachers' Kids and Missionaries' Kids) and a good chunk of folks who have enrolled in seminary classes. Only a third would describe themselves as American Baptists; a third describe themselves as formers (former Lutheran, former Catholic, former evangelical, former fundamentalist), and a third are seekers, or as some say, they landed at Judson for their last attempt at organized religion.

Despite all of Judson's potential and energy, the congregation was stuck, until it started moving. This is not a new idea. The great stories of the Bible are stories of movement: God saying to Abram, "Get you going." God instructing Moses, "Tell the Israelites to go forward" to cross the Red Sea. God leading Elijah, "Go now to Zarephath" and walk to the widow's home. Jesus walking in and around Galilee, preaching and teaching and healing and feeding. Paul's missionary journeys throughout the Mediterranean. The story of God is a story of movement.

Sometimes the movement is local; sometimes the movement is global. In movement the people of God find their mission (seek the welfare of the city), find their calling (you are a holy nation), and find their salvation (you have been healed, now go and do likewise). The challenge was/is/will always be how to be a movement while also being grounded. In the context of the local church, how do we function as a people on and of "The Way" while having a permanent address?

This is an honest book about pastoring in difficult times without all the answers. All I have is a deep trust that through moving and developing relationships, the way of God in this world will be made clearer. I confess I did not know how to connect or get to know the neighborhood Judson calls home. I knew in my bones, however, that the greatest loss for Judson was not the loss of membership but the loss of contact with our neighborhood. I have rolled my eyes repeatedly at church meetings and denominational conferences as presenters doled out their new catchphrases and surefire-winning methods. I rolled my eyes at them because on those occasions all they presented were great ideas with no concrete examples or possibilities. I will provide concrete ways for you to implement these ideas and provide ample room for you to find the way that works best in your local context. As you'll soon learn, you will become a local expert!

This book is not like a menu item from Applebee's; it is more like a sourdough starter (it will taste different in your context). I know that what works in Minneapolis might not work in Oakland or Detroit or Nashville, but the concepts in this book apply. At the end of each chapter, I provide an experiment for you to try, followed by study questions, suggested resources for further investigation, and a recipe. (Never separate church work from the stomach: Taste and see that the Lord is good.)

I have written this from a particular social position as a straight, temporarily able-bodied (TAB), middle-class, cisgender white male, which provides me advantages, privileges, and power that I neither earned nor deserve. In writing this book I am trying to use my advantages and privileges and power (and access to power) for the common good (Luke 12:48). For example, when I advocate for bike lanes, I am also advocating for complete streets, which means Americans with Disabilities Act–compliant sidewalks, more accessible public transit stops, and attention to immigrant voices and how minority communities experience interactions with the police on the street or public transit. All of these are intricately woven; this is not advocacy for the privileged, spandex-clad, speed-racing bicyclist. Rather, this is a book for pastors and engaged laity to invite and welcome movement into the lives of their congregations.

The modern church has been in a period of bewilderment, on a wayside, wondering where to go and how to get there. In 1971, Urban T. Holmes, then dean of Sewanee School of Theology, outlined the situation all modern church leaders experience on a daily basis. For 1,900 years, "it was assumed that we knew what we should be doing."[3] The inherited assumption is not so clear now: Folks do not naturally show up at church, become members, volunteer to serve on committees, tithe, teach Sunday School, read their Bible on a regular basis, and know how to pray. I have a shelf full of books that purport to reverse this trend, but by and large, they provide jogging-in-place approaches. The books entice the reader with the temptations to look busy and focus inward, change the church name, restructure the board, rewrite the bylaws—anything to avoid what we really need to do. The church needs to start moving, exploring, discovering; it needs to be surprised. It needs to walk, not talk. The church needs to venture out into our neighborhoods vulnerable, exposed, and with our guard down.

I know that venturing out into your neighborhood vulnerable, exposed, and with your guard down is a risky and even dangerous proposition. Yes, both my wife and sons have been hit by cars while riding their bikes. Yes, our bikes have been stolen. Yes, I have been in scary situations on the sidewalk and while on public transit. But those moments have not been the norm. The norm has been surprise, hospitality, compassion, and joy. And yes, I realize that as a straight, able-bodied, white male I operate with a level of privilege that others do not.

Nevertheless, what the world needs now is not a church (the building and the people) safely residing behind thick stone walls. The world needs people out in the community listening, catching stories, responding to, reacting to, and anticipating the needs and pains of the community. Sister Simone Campbell, former executive director of NETWORK, aka "Nuns on the Bus," once said, "Unless your heart is broken you're not gonna change your behavior. . . . You need to talk to some folks and hear their stories . . . and let your hearts be broken open . . . hear stories and you'll be changed."[4]

I propose we let our hearts be broken open by being a church on the move, literally. A church that promotes walking, bicycling, and taking public transit as the way for you to cross the threshold from the doors of the church into the doors in your neighborhood, parish, community. A church that, metaphorically, promotes movement into the neighborhood/parish as a way to reconnect with neighbors and renew church mission and ministry. Over time you will discover that the more you move out into your neighborhood/parish, just like a tide ebbs and flows, the more the neighborhood/parish will move into your congregation. There will be setbacks and resistance from both the congregation and the neighborhood, but as you build trust within the congregation and community, as you share stories, take risks, and reimagine ministry, you will experience the (re)discovery of the joy of ministry, the marriage of church renewal and social justice, and (re)connecting with your neighbors and neighborhood.

So, lace up your shoes, oil your chain, purchase a bus card, fill up your water bottle, grab a snack and a notebook, and let's get going.

May the words on these pages and the meditation of our hearts together be acceptable in thy sight, O God, our Rock and our Redeemer. Amen.

NOTES

1. This introduction is an expansion of an essay that originally appeared in *The Christian Century* as "Pastor on Two Wheels," November 14, 2014.

2. I wrote this quote while attending the lecture. I later asked Bill McKibben on Twitter if that is what he said. He replied, "definitely

sounds like me..." https://twitter.com/billmckibben/status/
1250207257595445250, 6:40 PM · April 14, 2020.

3. Urban T. Holmes III, *The Future Shape of Ministry* (New York: Seabury Press, 1971), 98.

4. Westminster Town Hall Forum, November 14, 2014, http://www
.westminsterforum.org/forum/nuns-on-the-bus-the-call-to-compassion/
found at 48:38–50:18.

Chapter 1
From Bikeable Parish to Church on the Move

On February 2, 2006, President George W. Bush invited Bono, lead singer of U2, to provide the National Prayer Breakfast remarks. Bono was asked to talk about the surprising work he and U.S. Sen. Jesse Helms did in the area of debt relief for poor nations. As he closed his talk, he told the story of a wise man that changed his life. "I was always seeking the Lord's blessing. I was saying, you know, I have a new song, look after it . . . I have a family, please look after them . . . I have this crazy idea . . . And then this wise man said: 'Stop.' He said, stop asking God to bless what you're doing. Get involved in what God is doing—because it's already blessed."[1]

I had prayed (and still do pray) Bono's prayer asking for God's blessing. But until this story I had not thought about God's activity in the community outside of the congregation I pastored. It seems silly, but it is true. This story started the process of giving me new eyes to see afresh the church's ministry. Once I started and once Judson Church started venturing out into the community (on foot, on bike, and aboard public transit), we found (unbeknownst to us) God at work. God is at work within my parish, within your parish, already blessing, already flourishing; it is our vocation as churches and as faith communities to discover that blessing and be a part of it.

Judson Church's Locale

Interstates 35W and 94 divide the rectangular boundaries of the city of Minneapolis into four quadrants. In each quadrant you will find a mix of wealthy homes, almost suburban neighborhoods, dense urban housing, racially and economically diverse areas, and some of the lakes that make up Minnesota's 10,000 lakes. In simple terms, most of south and northeast Minneapolis are primarily middle class to wealthy and white. The closer you get to downtown, the less wealthy and less white it becomes; north Minneapolis is primarily black and lower-income. Judson Church is in south Minneapolis, between I-35W and Lake Harriet. The immediate neighborhood is stable, residential, and mostly white, but the neighborhood borders a transition zone in economic and ethnic and density terms. Less than two miles east, George Floyd was killed; less than two miles north, a business corridor burned to the ground during the uprisings; and there are two homeless encampments in city parks within blocks of the church. It is situated in both an idyllic and challenging environment.

It took the congregation and me some time to get to know the community. I, for one, didn't know where to start. On a whim I called up the local city council member, Elizabeth Glidden, and asked if she could help me know my neighborhood better. She suggested I hang out at Curran's Restaurant, just around the corner from Judson. Confession: I did not want to hang out at Curran's. It is not a "foodie" place. They feature split pea soup and have daily senior specials and the aroma of corned beef lingers in the seats months after St. Patrick's Day. Yet Councilmember Glidden was spot on. Curran's has been a gold mine for me. The owners are committed to the community and social justice; it is affordable; and is easily the most diverse gathering in all of south Minneapolis. Once a week I go there for a cup of coffee or a $3 bowl of soup to watch, meet, and get to know people.[2]

Councilmember Gidden's advice was my start to getting into the community. I also found inspiration by following Dongho Chang, Seattle's chief traffic engineer, on Twitter (@dongho_chang). His Twitter feed is full of pictures of sidewalks, bike lanes, park benches, street signs, and public transit stops. It reveals how small changes to the urban environment make the city more livable, more accessible, and enjoyable. As you follow him, you quickly realize that this man does not work in an office much; he is always out and about walking, on his bike, or taking public transit.

Mr. Chang acts for me as a role model for the kind of pastor/ disciple the church on the move needs. A profile of him said as much: "Where some engineers (pastors and churches) get stuck in planning books (offices/studies, church buildings), Dongho is known for getting out into the community and trying out the things he helps to create."[3] Recently in Chicago for a conference, he dressed up for his presentation, then quickly changed into his bad-weather biking gear so he could get out and explore, see, and discover. Likewise, the more members of Judson are out in the community, the more stories we catch and share, which motivates other church members to go out and catch stories of their own. By getting out and exploring and seeing and discovering, we can envision ourselves as disciples of Jesus being sent out: curious inquirers seeking to learn and acquaint ourselves with our neighborhood and our city. Whereas Jesus sent out the twelve to proclaim, we are sent out to listen; instead of curing, we are seeing; instead of raising, we are catching; instead of cleansing, we are embracing; and instead of casting out, we are welcoming.[4]

The Parish Under My Nose

After my first year of bicycling year-round I was curious about how many miles I had logged. I installed a bicycle computer to keep track. I learned that the distance of the commute from my house to the church was 2.72 miles. I also noticed that most of my trips were less than three miles: to the hospital (2.8 miles), to parishioners' homes (0.5–3 miles), to the coffee shop (0.8 miles), to the bookstore (1.9 miles), to the Lutheran church to play basketball on Thursdays (4.8 miles). Although unscientific, my mileage logging proved to be spot on. The 2009 National Household Travel Survey revealed that 53 percent of all trips for Americans in urban areas were three miles or less; 44 percent were two miles or less; and 30 percent were less than one mile.[5]

This data was further analyzed in 2016 by the Federal Highway Administration, which found that 69.1 percent of trips two miles or less were done in cars.[6] This was a revelation to me: most of my trips are three miles or less.

From the beginning, I want you to see that walking or biking or taking public transit is an accomplishable goal. It makes sense to use a car for long-distance trips, but for short, everyday getting-around-town trips, cars aren't always necessary. A distance of one mile or less is a twenty-minute casual walk. A distance of two or three miles is an easy twenty-minute bike ride. I am not talking about riding your bike to IKEA (4.6 miles) to buy flat-pack furniture, or to Costco (10.6 miles) to stock up on forty-pound bags of dog food, or to Best Buy (4.2 miles) to purchase a flat-screen TV. (By the way, all those trips are bikeable for me.) But I am talking about the feasible/normal errands and trips (three miles or less) we make on a day-to-day basis.

For the next month, keep track of your daily drives. How many of your trips to church, school, grocery store, work, post office, doctor's office, library, dining out, or to the park are less than three miles? How many are less than one mile? Are 69.1 percent of your two-mile-or-less trips done by car? How close are you to public transit? What routes does it serve near you? Are there any bike lanes near you?

After you have compiled your list of daily trips for a month, think: How many could you walk instead? Bike instead? Use public transit instead?

All of my three-mile-or-less trips formed an imaginary boundary surrounding Judson Church. I wondered if there was a way to draw a three-mile circle on my computer with Judson at the center. Sure enough, there's an app for that, using Google Maps technology.

Having a picture of the area around Judson helped me visualize in a more systematic way what I saw each day when I walked,

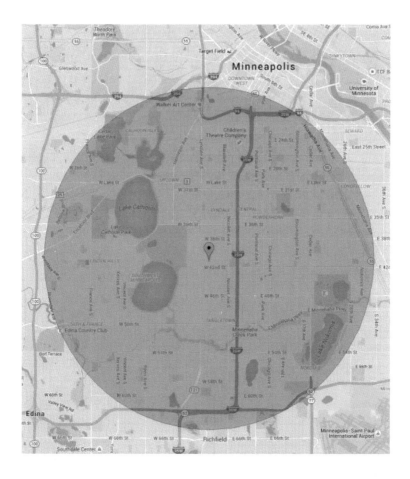

pedaled or took public transit. I started referring to the shaded area as "the bikeable parish," where any point from the center to the periphery is no farther than an easy twenty-minute bike ride.

My vision of a bikeable parish is an enlarged version of what urban planners call a "complete neighborhood." A complete neighborhood, or fifteen- to twenty-minute neighborhood, provides all of life's basic needs within a fifteen- to twenty-minute walk or bicycle ride from your house. The intent of a complete neighborhood and bikeable parish are the same as described by Daniel Herriges' Strong Towns blog post: "To break out of the mobility trap—the vicious cycle of driving ever-longer distances to get to the same things—and get back to building places around the most ancient, versatile, guaranteed-to-always-be-relevant transportation method there is: two legs. (And for those with disabilities, let's be clear that building for two legs and building for two wheels can and should go hand-in-hand.)"[7]

The Shift from Neighborhoods to Suburbs

How did we get from twenty-minute neighborhoods to suburbs and exurbs and destination churches? Most churches in America founded before or during World War I were started as parish or neighborhood churches within complete neighborhoods. They were planted to serve those who could walk, bike, or take the trolley there. If you can locate the earliest church directory for your church, the majority of the addresses will be within a few blocks of your church. After World War II, however, congregational life shifted from neighborhood-centered and walkable parishes to automobile-centered churches with wider, amorphous boundaries. This change was the result of two government initiatives: The Servicemen's Readjustment Act of 1944, or the GI Bill, which mandated that guaranteed home loans could be used only for new construction, and The Federal-Aid Highway Act of 1956, which encouraged and fueled the building of highways between major American cities, largely by placing eight lanes through their centers. Many times, these highways went in the path of least resistance, often through low-income and minority communities. It also did not help that in the 1930s, a subsidiary of General Motors bought up over one hundred streetcar companies and tore up 17,000 miles of tracks.[8] These initiatives favored new home construction (in the suburbs) over renting (in the city) and provided major roads out of the city. With mass-produced automobiles, good roads, and cheap gasoline, an individual or family could live in the suburbs and drive twenty, thirty or forty-five minutes to their "home church" in the city on Sunday mornings.

This change, initially, was fantastic for churches: membership swelled, programs excelled, and denominational structures grew and strengthened. But over the ensuing decades, the growth, excellence, and strength slowly crumbled. Churches that just fifty years ago had 1,200 on Sunday mornings now have 150. Some city-neighborhood churches have held on, while others relocated, merged, or closed. Researchers say between 3,000 and 10,000 churches in America close each year, with over 3,500 people leaving church each day.[9]

These are drastic and difficult times, where the conditions for survival are front and center. It may feel like we need to shore up what we have and preserve it, but that will only prolong a sure and certain demise. In many ways our time mirrors the second century, when the early church battled with Gnosticism. Gnosticism taught that Jesus provided salvation not by his life, teachings, practices, death, and resurrection but by revealing esoteric knowledge, or gnosis. According to Charles Foster, in his book *The Sacred Journey*, the church adopted the practice of pilgrimage (i.e., movement) as a defense against Gnosticism to prevent it from becoming stale and inflexible.[10]

When the church started to become inwardly focused, that was the precise time it needed to start moving. In the midst of global crises of climate change, health pandemic, economic disparity and immigration, in the midst of national crises of race relations and violence, in the midst of declining church membership and attendance, the church needs to start moving once again.

The movement I am proposing is not a pilgrimage to Rome but becoming pilgrims in your neighborhood/community/parish as a way to get to know those who are also moving to your town/city/urban center. Already around you is movement, a mass migration to and around urban areas. Professors Byron Stone and Claire Wolfteich of the Boston University School of Theology provide embryonic examples of city-neighborhood churches staying planted but being open to movement with their 2008 book *Sabbath in the City: Sustaining Urban Pastoral Excellence*. Their research revealed that "urban churches (which) are intentional about remaining and thriving in the city must be committed and open to change. Indeed, some of the congregations that not only survive but thrive in the city have come to see their relationship to the ever-changing urban context as pilgrimages— as an opportunity to be embraced hopefully rather than an obstacle to be hurdled."[11] As urban and neighborhood churches become ever more vital to the spiritual health of their communities, Stone and Wolfteich stress, pastors and congregations need to incorporate a "willingness to learn new things, to visit other churches, and to explore new ideas, strategies, paradigms, and approaches to key areas of ministry."[12]

The Original Blessing: An Old Idea Revisited

Originally Judson Church was an expression of movement, a mission/chapel founded by Calvary Baptist in 1909 on what was then prairie with undeveloped lots, dirt roads, and a trolley line. In 1909 there were only two churches in the neighborhood: Incarnation Roman Catholic Church and Judson Memorial Baptist Church. That's right, the Baptists and Catholics predated the Lutherans in south Minneapolis![13] The church quickly grew to 500, peaked at 1,200 in the 1940s and early '50s, then began its gradual decline to today's membership of 225 with an average of 110 on Sunday mornings. Our story is the story of most American city-neighborhood churches. Judson is not a neighborhood church anymore; we're a destination congregation with a building in south Minneapolis and a membership from around the metro area. Or at least that's what we thought.

My daily trips were telling me that the majority of the Judson Church community lived within the bikeable parish, but the members of Judson were saying the church was a destination congregation that drew from around the metropolitan area. Indeed, we do have members who drive fifteen, twenty, twenty-five, even forty miles on Sunday mornings to be a part of the church. But they are not the norm. No matter how many times I said this, people didn't believe me. Luckily, I discovered another app that allowed me to upload the church directory and pin each address onto a Google map (first I had to convert the directory from a PDF to a Word document, then into an Excel document, then save it as a CSV file). Instantly, a map of the whole Judson community appeared. A simpler way to do this is to give the youth a hard copy of your church directory and a few sheets of small round stickers and let them attach the stickers to an old wall map of your community that is, more than likely, hanging in an old Sunday School room, to create an analog version of the Google map.

The app revealed what my walking, pedaling, and public transiting had been telling me: Around 70 percent of the Judson community lived within the three-mile area. Yes, people do drive from all over the metropolitan area to be a part of Judson, but they are not the majority. The Judson norm, in fact, is the American norm; according to a recent study by Baylor University, almost 70 percent of Americans drive fifteen minutes or less to attend weekly worship services.

Don't Forget the 30 Percent!

In 1914, when the cornerstone for Judson Church was laid, it was remarked that the church's leading characteristics were "freedom of thought, democratic brotherliness, and high spiritual purpose." Those characteristics still guide the church today, along with our three core values: creative, relational, and inclusive.

We are also a Welcoming and Affirming congregation and we love our choir, pipe organ, and traditional music. Each week someone from the community offers a personal reflection, aka testimony; we recognize our white privilege and are working on racial reconciliation; we support women in ministry; we incorporate the arts (one member wrote a requiem that the choir performed, and another member wrote a rock opera the church performed); and we attempt to accommodate members of all abilities. All to say we will always attract members from outside the three-mile zone. In fact, the original church directory proved it! The zone is an imaginary demarcation, not an impenetrable wall.

Our values and characteristics and commitments are what the individuals and families need to be healthy and whole and loving people of God, and Judson needs them as much as they need Judson. Nevertheless, expect some pushback on shifting from a metro-defined, car-centric community to a bikeable parish. I heard more than once, "If you don't live near the church, the church doesn't care about you." Ironically, the more neighborhood-focused we have become, the more I have heard inquiries and desires from those living outside the three-mile circle about moving closer to the church. The core of the resistance was not because of our ministry-focused locale, but more because of the change from serving the church members first to serving the community first.

The 2017 Baylor study also revealed "the gap between a person's place of residence and their place of worship has implications.[14]

"As the distance from a congregation increases, the likelihood of weekly attendance decreases." The study also revealed that "the people most satisfied with their neighborhood are those who attend congregations in their neighborhood." Here is where technology can help strengthen the ties that bind. Weekly emails, Facebook posts, congregation-wide weekly prayer on Wednesdays at noon, and video links can help with frayed relations due to distance. We are also developing intentional gatherings for the 30 percent and those who live alone as a way to strengthen both. We will always be a hybrid church with a majority living in the city and a significant minority driving in from a good distance. Once we recognized this, we were able to adapt, create, and plan our model for ministry.

Richard Rohr, discussing original sin in his book *The Universal Christ*, says, "If you start with a problem, you tend to never get beyond that mindset."[15] Throughout my twenty years of being a pastor, I have focused on the problem: The church is dying and it is happening on my watch! No matter how clever, spiritual, or original my ideas were, they all focused on the problem. Then I began to see anew that my focus as a pastor was not to solve the problem but to see the blessing. Judson Church's original orientation was a city-neighborhood church—walkable, bikeable, public transit-able; that was its original blessing. It is my job as pastor in this parish to find God already at work within it and discover ways for Judson to partner with others to lift up the original blessing as lived in the 2020s.

As we envision this new way of being a people of faith, let us be inspired by this simple line adapted from the preface of *The Rule of St. Benedict*, written 1,500 years ago: *In drawing up this model, I hope to set down nothing harsh, nothing burdensome. May it be so. Amen.*

Experiment: Alley Walk

One day at the coffee shop I discovered a map of artist Rachel Breen's murals of heirloom seeds on garage doors in Minneapolis' Kingfield neighborhood, where Judson is located. One sunny Sunday I invited folks from Judson to join me as we walked around the neighborhood and viewed the garage doors. As we ambled up and down the alleyways, we realized that we were doing more than just viewing garage doors; we were discovering our neighborhood. If we had gone up and down the sidewalks and knocked on front doors, we would have gotten nowhere.

But in the alleyway, we were met with curious and friendly faces. One neighbor had no idea there were murals on garage doors, another neighbor offered us lemonade, and another neighbor was moving in and asked us if we could recommend a place for ice cream! One Sunday after worship, for thirty minutes, walk the alleyways around your church and note what you see and who you meet.

Questions for Further Reflection

1. Draw your parish: What are its boundaries? Who calls it home? What brings joy to those who call it home? What causes pain in the parish?

2. How is your church/faith community a good neighbor in the parish?

3. How does your church's origin story or stories impact its present life?

4. Could you tithe your trips? Could you for one month walk, bike, or take public transit for 10 percent of your trips?

5. How would tithing your trips cause you to suffer and at the same time cause others more joy?

6. When was the last time you walked around your neighborhood? Rode your bike? Boarded a bus, light rail, or the train?

7. Describe your church/faith community in terms of a field hospital rather than a mighty fortress.

8. What tours could you organize or participate in for your parish? Garden tours? Art tours? Bike tour? Walking tour? Library tour? School tour? Park tour?

9. How does the interstate in your city impact neighborhood life?

10. Where is God already at work in your parish?

Suggested Reading List

Everett, Laura. *Holy Spokes: The Search for Urban Spirituality on Two Wheels*. Grand Rapids, MI: Eerdmans, 2017. This book provides a broader picture of bicycling and faith practices.

Johnson, D.B. *Eddie's Kingdom*. Boston, MA: HMH, 2005. A picture book illustrating how one child through his art creates a community in an apartment complex.

Sparks, Paul, Soerens, Tim and Friesen, Dwight J. *The New Parish: How Neighborhood Churches are Transforming Mission, Discipleship and Community*. Downers Grove, IL: IVP, 2014. Although they define parish differently than I do, their book is helpful for establishing how we re-appropriate parish for contemporary experience.

Bartlett, Gene E. *The Authentic Pastor*. Valley Forge, PA: Judson, 1978. The book I go back to time and time again to remind me how to be a city-neighborhood pastor.

Van Gelder, Craig. "Effects of Auto-Mobility on Church Life and Culture," *Word & World* Vol. 28, No. 3, Summer 2008. Fantastic historical article.

Recipe: 100 Mile Granola

While walking, biking, or taking public transit in your parish, no doubt you stopped by a local farmers market to see what's in season and what your local farmers are growing and harvesting. Here is a recipe I developed using ingredients grown within one hundred miles of Judson Church. Feel free to adapt it using ingredients you find farmers are growing in your area.

4 cups rolled oats
1 cup toasted buckwheat groats (these take the place of almonds in my granola; toasting them provides a nutty flavor and crunch)
⅓ cup toasted sunflower seeds
⅓ cup toasted millet
⅓ cup flaxseed
1 tsp salt
¼ cup sunflower oil
¼ cup unsalted butter
¼ cup maple syrup
¼ cup honey

Preheat oven to 300 degrees.

Line a baking sheet with parchment paper.

Mix together the dry ingredients in a large bowl and set aside.

In a saucepan over medium heat, combine the wet ingredients and stir for three minutes or until blended.

Pour the melted mixture over the oat mixture and stir till coated evenly. Spread the granola mixture evenly on the baking sheet.

Bake for 25–35 minutes, stirring every 10 minutes, until granola is a deep brown. Let the mixture cool to room temperature before eating.

Store in a mason jar and enjoy.

This makes a great pre-ride breakfast with yogurt and an even better snack while walking, riding, or taking public transit.

NOTES

1. Bono, Keynote Address at the 54th National Prayer Breakfast, Americanrhetoric.com, February 2, 2006, http://www.americanrhetoric.com/speeches/bononationalprayerbreakfast.htm.

2. Sadly Curran's closed in August 2020, a victim of the pandemic. The restaurant has since been torn down and is being redeveloped as an apartment complex.

3. David Gutman, "Meet the man striving to make Seattle's streets safer, more efficient," Traffic Lab profile, *Seattle Times*, December 4, 2017, https://www.seattletimes.com/seattle-news/transportation/meet-the-man-transforming-seattle-one-curb-at-a-time/.

4. Matthew 10:7-8, "As you go, proclaim the good news, 'The kingdom of heaven has come near.' Cure the sick, raise the dead, cleanse the lepers, cast out demons," *The Green Bible: The New Revised Standard Version* (HarperOne: San Francisco. 2008).

5. Darren Flusche, "National Household Travel Survey—Short Trips Analysis," The League of American Bicyclists, January 22, 2010, http://bikeleague.org//content/national-household-travel-survey-short-trips-analysis.

6. Lisa Halverstadt, "Driving When You Could Bike Fact Check," voiceofsandiego.org, March 20, 20213, https://www.voiceofsandiego.org/topics/news/driving-when-you-could-bike-fact-check/.

7. Daniel Herriges, "7 Rules for Creating '15-Minute Neighborhoods,'" strongtowns.org, September 6, 2019, https://www.strongtowns.org/journal/2019/9/6/7-rules-for-creating-15-minute-neighborhoods. Also, explore one of *Time* magazine's lists of "The 100 Most Influential People of 2020," September 22, 2020, and you will find Paris mayor Anne Hidalgo and her efforts to transform the City of Lights into a large series of connected complete neighborhoods, https://time.com/collection/100-most-influential-people-2020/5888321/anne-hidalgo/.

8. Joseph Stromburg, "The real story behind the demise of America's once-mighty streetcars," vox.com, May 7, 2015, https://www.vox.com/2015/5/7/8562007/streetcar-history-demise.

9. Ryan Sheehan, "3500 People Leave the Church Every Day," *The Christian Post*, May 27, 2015, https://www.christianpost.com/news/3500-people-leave-the-church-every-day-139631/.

10. Charles Foster, *The Sacred Journey* (Nashville: Thomas Nelson, 2010), 19. "Pilgrimage, done properly, is one of the best-known antidotes to gnosticism."

11. Byron P. Stone and Claire E. Wolfteich, *Sabbath in the City: Sustaining Urban Pastoral Excellence* (Louisville, KY: Westminster John Knox Press, 2008), 8.

12. Ibid, 9.

13. See https://en.wikipedia.org/wiki/Demographics_of_Minnesota. This is saying something in a state where Lutherans now make up 24 percent and Baptists account for 5 percent of Minnesotans.

14. Kevin D. Dougherty, "Location, Location, Location," chapter IV in *American Values, Mental Health, and Using Technology in the Age of Trump,* Findings from the Baylor Religion Survey, Wave 5, September 2017, 55–59, https://www.baylor.edu/baylorreligionsurvey/doc.php/292546.pdf.

15. Richard Rohr, *The Universal Christ: How a Forgotten Reality Can Change Everything We See, Hope for, and Believe* (New York: Convergent, 2019), 62.

Chapter 2
Parking

*E*very time I proposed that Judson Church needed to move out into the community, I felt the presence of fear both in the hearts of the congregation and in mine. I kept hearing the same three fear-filled reasons why our venturing out into the community would fail: one, we did not have enough parking for visitors and new members; two, we did not have the resources to attract and keep visitors and new members; and three, there was not enough time to turn the church around so that we could attract and keep new members. Over the next three chapters I will show how you can introduce movement into these three areas. I know it may seem odd to think you can incorporate movement into parking, resources, and time, but then again you probably didn't think walking, bicycling, and taking public transit could renew your church either! I want to start with parking because if you can transform your vision of parking, then your other resources (primarily staff and the building) and time are a piece of cake.

In the spring of 1988, the Rev. Walt Pulliam concluded his thirteen-year pastorate at Judson Church and retired from full-time pastoral ministry. Weeks before he preached his last sermon, he told the congregation he would use the opportunity to share his word of wisdom for the future of Judson. For weeks, congregants wondered what word Rev. Pulliam would share. For his last sermon he told the congregation the essence of their future hung on one word. That word was PARKING. If only Judson could acquire space for parking, then folks could drive in from miles around and easily park, and the church's future would be secured.

Rev. Pulliam had every right to believe in the promise of parking. During his tenure at Judson, he watched two nearby congregations, Bethlehem Lutheran (two blocks west of Judson) and Mount Olivet Lutheran (a mile southwest of Judson and supposedly the largest ELCA congregation in North America) grow by leaps and bounds. Both started, like Judson, as city-neighborhood churches, both had talented pastors, beautiful buildings, gifted musicians, engaged leadership, and visions for ministry (if anything, Judson Church probably had more "church talent" than the other two). But there was one thing the Lutheran congregations had that Judson did not: parking. As Judson's footprint remained the same, the membership contracted, but as Mount Olivet's and Bethlehem's footprints grew, so did their membership—especially when they bought the lots around them and turned them into impervious asphalt surfaces for automobile parking spaces (89 for Bethlehem, 332 for Mount Olivet; yes, I counted—while riding my bike). Today these Lutheran congregations have at least five services each Sunday and multiple campuses in the area, own and operate year-round camps, nursing homes, and counseling centers, and offer a plethora of excellent ministries and services.

From the outside it appears God blessed Mount Olivet and Bethlehem Lutheran and let Judson Church wither. What if we removed ourselves from the competitive realm (there are no winners and losers in the Kingdom of God), and saw the lack of parking as a different kind of blessing?

Meditation: What Is a Church Parking Lot?

Remember, churches survived, succeeded, and even flourished 1,900 years before parking lots ever existed. In fact, most city-neighborhood churches never had parking lots or spaces at their genesis.[1] The need for church parking lots emerged only after most of the members moved to the suburbs, away from the city-neighborhood church, and drove in for Sunday worship services. Before they drove and parked, most congregations walked, biked, or took public transit to church.

For a moment, contemplate a parking lot. What is it exactly? A parking lot is a flat, impervious surface with one purpose and one purpose only: the temporary (at most, a few hours one day a week) storage of automobiles. Automobile spaces can be used only by those who can drive, excluding children, a good number of seniors, and those physically unable. It is a dedicated resource of precious space and money that is not equally used by those who walk, bicycle, take public transit or those who cannot drive.

A church parking lot is something more too. I invite you to stand in a church parking lot or close your eyes and envision standing in a church parking lot. Notice the distance between yourself and neighboring houses, local businesses or passersby. You are standing on a horizontal wall, an asphalt expanse that disconnects your faith community from the neighbors and community where it abides.

As an experiment, take a sheet of paper and recreate the houses, businesses, or parks that used to be where your church parking lot is now. How many houses/businesses/trees did it usurp? Or to illustrate how far removed you are from your neighbors, one Sunday after worship, form a human chain in the church parking lot. Holding hands, start from the door everyone uses to enter the church from the parking lot out to the main street. How many people does it take to cross this distance?

A church parking lot can be a public good (as we will see) but for the moment, consider how it enables your church to be disconnected from the community where it is located. It enables people from outside the church's neighborhood to drive in from other neighborhoods without ever connecting with the church's neighbors or neighborhood. You may think a church parking lot is neutral at worst, positive at best for your congregation. But most, if not all, church parking lots enable your church to function as a de-neighborhood church, where "the proximity that characterized the neighborhood church is gone, and with it informal dimensions of community that reinforced the ideas of religion, indeed made it possible to talk about partnership between home, school and church in ways about which we can only reminisce."[2] The change associated with removing the church membership from the neighborhood is similar to what happens in the insect world: "If you remove caterpillars from a given habitat, you are not left with the same environment minus caterpillars. You have a new environment and have reconstituted the conditions for survival."[3]

The new environment a church parking lot creates is a de-neighborhood church with members who drive in from other neighborhoods and have little or no connection to neighbors or the neighborhood the church inhabits. It doesn't have to be this way. What if church parking lots functioned more like bridges than walls? What if a church parking lot functioned more like a plaza where the faith community re-neighbors itself to its once-familiar home?[4]

Parking: Seeking the Perfect Spot

No one knows how many parking spaces exist in America; estimates range from one billion to two billion to three billion. There are, however, approximately 275 million registered automobiles. That means there are about four or eight or twelve parking spots per registered automobile in America.[5] Regardless of which number is most accurate, that is a lot (pun intended) of 200-square-foot areas (the average parking space measures 20 feet by 10 feet) devoted to the temporary storage of automobiles. The Rev. Pamela Fickenscher and William Schroeer illustrate why this devoted and dedicated space for temporary automobile storage is not just a practical land land-use issue but also reveals an unjust priority of Christian communities. "Each car turns out to require roughly eight parking spaces—not only at home, at work, the store, the park, the school, but for many, many congregations, a spot at church. Parking at church is not just about where you and your parishioners put your cars. It is about how a Christian community determines who gets the easiest access from the outside of the building to the inside. It is about the relationships with neighbors, often including some who would prefer the church not be there at all. It is about how we care for the two-thirds of people in the United States who are most vulnerable and don't drive: children and the elderly. It is about how we care for God's creation, and what we do about the pollutants produced by all those cars driving to church."[6]

It is not difficult to imagine a time you circled a block two, three, four, or even five times trying to find the perfect parking spot. Most of the traffic and most of the air pollution caused by automobiles in American cities emerges from drivers just like you and me trying to find the perfect parking spot. And where is the perfect parking spot? It's right up front, as close as possible to the door of the grocery store, theater, church, bank, or coffee shop. When we find the perfect parking spot, we feel like we won the lottery. Perhaps you recall the *Seinfeld* episode when George Costanza visited friends who had a baby and found a perfect parking spot in front of the hospital. Once in the room, George asked mom and dad if they would like to join him at the window so he could show the new baby the perfect parking spot as an inspiration.[7]

Why do we spend so much time and energy looking for "the perfect parking spot"? Temporarily able-bodied people[8] will circle the block for twenty minutes looking for the closest spot at the mall, only to walk several thousand steps while inside the mall shopping (the Centers for Disease Control and Prevention even has a Mall Walking program).[9] We look for the closest spot because parking lots are boring at best (asphalt and yellow lines) and dangerous at worst (no safe walkways).

A Church Plaza: Beyond the Perfect Spot

In the spring of 2019 people in San Francisco realized it was cheaper to pay for public parking spots than to rent office space. As an experiment, workers fed parking meters with coins, set up tables and chairs, and created outdoor workspaces. They announced via Twitter, using the hashtag #WePark, to link with others throughout the city. The movement quickly spread to other cities and across Europe. Those participating were challenging both the high cost of office rental space and the amount of space we devote to automobiles rather than people. As the experiment grew those participating also discovered how isolated and alone they felt and how much they missed working in a community.[10]

Individuals in your community may not be working in parking spaces but there is a good chance that on the third Friday of September, you can see some alternative ideas for parking spaces. That's International Park(ing) Day, deemed so by the American Society of Landscape Artists (ASLA). On this day the ASLA encourages people from around the globe to transform public parking spaces into uses other than the temporary storage of automobiles. "Urban inhabitants worldwide recognize the need for new approaches to making the urban landscape, and realize that converting small segments of the automobile infrastructure—even temporarily—can alter the character of the city. From public parks to free health clinics, from art galleries to demonstration gardens, *PARK(ing) Day* participants have claimed the metered parking space as a rich new territory for creative experimentation and activism."[11]

Some cities are encouraging "longer than a day" approaches for these parking spaces as they experiment with temporary, seasonal mini-parks or "parklets" that fit inside the space of a parking spot and contain places for people to sit, stand, and move about. Restaurants have used parking spaces to provide more outdoor seating. We have seen this especially as restaurants and businesses have adapted to the restraints of COVID-19. Overnight, parking spots were transformed into outdoor dining areas.

Why couldn't churches do likewise? Can you envision a parklet with a few chairs and a couple of tables for neighbors to congregate and have coffee? Or envision a seasonal outdoor parklet-chapel—an intimate holy place to rest, pray, and meditate, like way stations along ancient pilgrimage routes? When I offered this idea to a local architect, his eyes got big as he quickly scribbled on a napkin a mini-Gothic cathedral with colored plexiglass windows to replicate stained glass.

Joel Karsten of Roseville, Minnesota, wanted to start a vegetable garden at his new home, but his soil was poor and thin. Joel didn't have the money to build raised beds, but he did have a memory of healthy and vigorous thistles growing out of straw bales from his time growing up on a dairy farm in southwestern Minnesota. He started experimenting with growing vegetables in straw bales. It took years of failures and successes, but he perfected the art of straw bale gardening.

The amazing aspect of straw bale gardening is that you do not need any soil, only five to eight hours of sun every day. In one church parking space, you can fit twenty straw bales directly on top of the asphalt. These twenty straw bales can yield enough produce to feed a family of four throughout the summer and fall. Imagine the symbolism of a church giving up two parking spaces to grow vegetables and giving the food away to a food shelf or soup kitchen—enough food to feed eight to ten people! Or imagine the church inviting people from the neighborhood to establish a community garden in some of your parking spaces.

In a similar vein, city-neighborhood churches around North America are giving away their parking spaces on Saturday mornings to local farmers markets. For a few hours on Saturday mornings, a lifeless expanse of asphalt becomes a joyous, boisterous community. Other churches have painted a labyrinth on their lots, blocked the entrances on weeknights, and invited the community for an evening of contemplation. Other churches have blocked off their parking lots for extended periods of time, so neighborhood kids have a safe place to play. Michele Molstead, former outreach director at NiceRide, a bike-share company in the Twin Cities, suggested a new model for VBS (Vacation Bible School) as Vacation Bike School, where city-neighborhood church parking lots are used to teach kids, immigrant communities, non-spandex-clad young adults, and interested seniors how to ride bikes, bike safety, and bike repair. Church parking lots were repurposed during COVID-19 into community dinner sites, drive-in theaters, COVID-19 testing sites, ballot drop-off sites, trick or treat venues, drive-in concert and Christmas pageant stages, and more.

Pete Seeger wrote on his banjo's head, "This Machine Surrounds Hate and Forces It to Surrender." An assistant dean at New York University, David Hollander, thinks the same sentiment can be said for basketball. His course "How Basketball Can Save the World" lifts up the democratic, accessible, and cooperative aspects of basketball. Imagine city-neighborhood churches following Dr. Hollander's lead and transforming parking plazas into basketball courts.

In the late 1980s, someone—no one, to this day, knows who—in the outskirts of St. Albans, West Virginia, my hometown, installed nine-foot basketball rims in the church parking lot of a Methodist church. Within days word had spread throughout the town about the presence of nine-foot rims (regulation basketball rims are ten feet). From after school until dusk and starting early in the morning on weekends, kids, up to one hundred at a time, waited patiently to play on this court and for their chance to dunk a basketball. The Methodist church was sitting on an outreach gold mine! After a few weeks of our daily presence, the church, rather than welcome us as the strangers in their midst, began to run us off. Then one mournful day, someone from the church came with a blowtorch and cut the basketball poles down to the ground. In the church's mind, the basketball court was a parking lot, reserved for the cars of drivers not from the neighborhood; it was not a plaza to be shared and enjoyed by the neighbors (especially those ages 12–15).

Church parking lots can be more than sources of food, prayer, fun, and exercise; they can also be sources of housing. Churches in the San Francisco Bay area have invited people who live in their cars to park in their parking lots for the night. These churches provide more than a 20-by-10-foot space; they also provide safety, along with kitchen, bathroom and laundry access, and a sense of community. Some churches throughout the nation are going further, seeking to transform their 20-by-10 spaces into lots for tiny homes. In many locations, churches are exempt from some zoning laws, so their parking lots are the only locations in urban environments where tiny homes can be placed. Some of the tiny homes function as transitional housing, while others function as permanent residences.

In south Minneapolis, Calvary Lutheran Church on 39th Street and Chicago Avenue, one block south of where George Floyd was killed, transformed their church parking lot into a community center, offering food, clothing, medical supplies, and water. As the days of street protests turned into weeks their parking lot hosted voter registration drives and functioned as a staging area for protesters and marches.

In north Minneapolis, Don and Sondra Samuels felt a desire to do something with the rage, pain, and lament their community was experiencing after the killing of George Floyd. Their vision was for a pop-up prayer tent in the community; they chose an abandoned parking lot. They transformed the lot on West Broadway and Bryant Avenue into a spiritual healing center. The tent was not a backyard pop-up tent but a grand structure that had the look of a tent revival. It was a revival, but of a different kind; a moral revival, an anti-racism revival, a revival led by black preachers and artists to show the way for the white community. Instead of preaching, there was silent prayer. Instead of pews, there were pillows and chairs. Instead of a "come to Jesus" moment, there was a "come to your senses" moment, a call for transformation. Instead of music used to manipulate your emotions, there was a singing bowl. Instead of the "four steps to salvation," there was an invitation to repair the brokenness. Instead of stained glass, there were creations by local artists that were being completed before your eyes. I imagine it was what a revival would have looked like if Howard Thurman, ever planned one. The parking lot became a holy, transformative, and promising space.

If faith communities could only slightly shift their gaze from parking lots as temporary automobile storage to functioning more like plazas, they could see a new world blossom before their eyes. Parking lots have one function and one function only: temporary automobile storage. But a plaza has multiple functions; you can temporarily park a car on it and abundantly more!

Less Is More: What If You Do Not Have a Parking Lot?

Author and farmer Gene Logsdon, a self-described contrary farmer, provided me the lens to see the abundance of parking. In his book *The Contrary Farmer*, Logsdon reveals how on his small farm dedicated to organic principles and crop rotation, one can out-produce per acre gigantic monoculture farms. Because he plants two or three crops per year on the same acre of land, his bounty is plentiful, whereas monoculture farmers only plant and harvest one crop per year. Not wanting to go into debt and take risks beyond his comfort level, Logsdon imposed limitations on his land that caused him to think creatively about the use of his farm and production.[12]

It may seem odd to pull from the work of farmers in rural lands for urban inspiration, but it should come as no surprise to urban and neighborhood churches that our day-to-day existence vacillates between the Garden of Eden and the City of God. On Sunday morning at worship, we sing "Savior, Like a Shepherd Lead Us" or "Now the Green Blade Riseth," then on Monday evening at church council meetings, we discuss gentrification and how to help those experiencing homelessness. On Tuesday morning at Bible study, we discuss the parable of the sower, then walk out to a neighborhood with underfunded public schools. Logsdon even coined a new word to describe the blending of rural and urban worlds: "rurban." I think it wonderfully explains neighborhood and urban churches' existence.

Throughout the years Judson Church has tried to acquire land around the church to create a parking lot. In the 1990s, the church was able to purchase a house next to the church. The church planned to demolish the house and create a parking lot. After the purchase, an architect revealed to Judson they could carve out only six parking places, at most. That revealed a broader problem: For Judson to obtain enough off-street parking to accommodate a healthy Sunday attendance, the church would have to acquire, tear down, and pave over eight houses on Harriet Avenue. This act would have radically transformed the nature of the neighborhood so that Judson Church could satisfy its need for the temporary storage of cars for a few hours, one day a week. The church abandoned its dream of acquiring off-street parking and, I believe, its dream of becoming a flourishing congregation.

But there is another way. In 2012 the Australian organization Cycling Promotion Fund made a public demonstration to show the greater efficiency of walking, biking, and taking public transit to get from point A to point B. In the space taken by 60 cars, roads can accommodate sixteen buses or six hundred bicycles or almost one thousand pedestrians.[13]

| 60 people | 60 people and 1 bus | 60 people and 60 bikes | 60 people and 60 cars |

By focusing efforts more on those who can walk, bike, or take public transit, rather than only those who drive, Judson Church saw it did not need a parking lot. In fact, we had all the parking we needed.

Judson Church has thirteen on-street automobile parking spots. Inside just one 20-by-10-foot automobile parking spot, ten bikes can be parked. This bike rack in the outline of a car, aka a car-shaped bike port, designed by the British company Cycle-hoop, provides a visual example of ten bikes easily parked in one parking space.

(photo credit: Cyclehoop Ltd)

Judson also has eight spots of boulevard bike parking, which could easily expand to forty or fifty more with permanent racks, or on Sunday mornings, we could use temporary bike racks like the ones used for triathlons or other biking events in lieu of on-street automobile parking spots.

In an effort to increase the availability of bicycle parking, the city of Minneapolis entered into an agreement with a local bike parking manufacturer, Dero. Local businesses and the city jointly purchase bicycle parking racks, each paying 50 percent of the cost. Local businesses pay for installation. Although this agreement is unique to the Twin Cities, there is potential for it to be duplicated with other manufacturers and local governments around the nation.

Brompton Bikes UK asked the question: How many foldable bikes could fit in the space of one car parking spot, 20 feet by 10 feet? The answer is forty-two.

(photo credit: Brompton Bicycle Ltd)

You have an abundance of parking, but how can you get people to recognize it and begin to utilize it?

Indeed, not everyone will be able to walk, bike, or take public transit. Some cannot drive, some live too far away, others have physical limitations. Too many times, however, churches have prioritized able-bodied drivers over the rest of the congregation. Imagine a congregation adopting a movement of solidarity where a small group of able-bodied drivers is asked to neither drive alone, nor park near the front of the church, nor drive at all, if that is an option. The goal is for a core of able-bodied people within the faith community to explore and employ alternative transit options. This may seem like an incredible request but imagine the impact when able-bodied drivers are in solidarity with the two-thirds of the congregation that cannot drive (children, some seniors, and those who are physically unable). This small act of solidarity on Sunday mornings can create small connections of empathy and compassion, making the heart a little more tender. Just as Jesus proclaimed in his day, *blessed are the most vulnerable* (the widow, children, those with physical limitations, those who were socially ostracized), so too can the church today proclaim this same blessing with its alternative emphasis on transit and parking.

Even if only five parking spaces are freed up because of this commitment, that is five spaces that were not previously available for the elderly or those with physical challenges to be more of a part of the faith community they love. As more people walk, bike, or take public transit, more parking spots will be made available, enabling the faith community to see the abundance of parking and become more creative about the available parking spots. In many cities, unfortunately, there is not frequent public transit service on Sunday mornings.

Churches, however, have options:

1. Churches could move their worship/gathering time to another day when public transit is more reliable. Our common experience of COVID-19 has revealed a variety of worship times and possibilities as individuals and families choose when and how they worship. Could a post-COVID-19 church allow for a central worship time other than Sunday morning?

2. Neighboring churches along public transit routes could lobby together and request that their local transit authorities increase Sunday service.

3. Faith communities could band together to revive the model of the church van as a faith-community-public-transit alternative. In a good-faith effort, churches could offer staggered start times, similar to many urban school schedules, to make sharing a van even easier.

4. Churches could use Google Maps as shown in Chapter 1 to plan efficient carpooling scenarios.

Parking lots can be turned into plazas, and not having a parking lot is not a curse. By starting with and focusing on parking, we can discover ways to move into the community. When Rev. Pulliam emphasized *parking* as the key to the church's future, he was spot on. He knew, like all of us know, that when a church has a committee or business meeting, there are really two meetings that take place: the real one that is scheduled and takes place in the designated meeting room, and the really real one that takes place after the meeting in the parking lot or on the sidewalk. Maybe our churches are telling us something about where our energy and efforts should be placed.

In the Spirit of the Prayer of St. Francis

Lord, make parking an instrument of thy peace. Where there is scarcity, let there be abundance.
Where there is only the temporary storage of automobiles, let there be a multi-use plaza.
Where there is only parking, let there be tiny houses.
Where there is only parking, let there be a community garden.
Where there is only parking, let there be a labyrinth.
Where there is only parking, let there be a bicycle training course.
Where there is only parking, let there be basketball, kickball, pickleball, street hockey, and soccer playing surfaces.
O Master, let us not seek parking as much as to be more park-like, to welcome the neighbors and neighborhood, not shun them, to be a bridge into the community, not protected behind a horizontal wall.
For it is in giving up the false promise that parking will make all of our church problems go away that a small city-neighborhood church can experience abundant life. Amen.

Experiment: Public Transit Ride

Ask around in your congregation to find out who is familiar with public transit in your neighborhood or city. Then ask if they would serve as a guide for a group from your church. The goal is to get people who have never ridden public transit to do so in a group setting with trusted friends. If no one from your church is familiar with public transit, call the transit authority and ask if they can send a representative or a transit ambassador to your church after worship one Sunday.

A few weeks ahead of your "Transit Sunday Tour," plan your loop route with your guide/ambassador. For our rides at Judson, I like to include at least two transfers, so folks can familiarize themselves with getting on and off different buses. I also include a local restaurant as our midway stop, with a park or historic district nearby to stroll after lunch.

Before leaving church, ask each participant to write down three or four sentences about what they expect to experience (will they be safe? Are they nervous?). After the ride, give them a worksheet with these questions:

How easy was it to find the bus? Get on the bus? Pay for your ride?

What did you notice while you rode? What parts of the neighborhood or city did you see that you had not seen before?

What was it like to arrive at a destination without looking for parking? Without being in control of the route or speed? If you had driven, how would the experience have been different?

Who else was on the bus/light rail/streetcar? Who did you share space with? How many languages did you hear?

Describe the people you recall who got off and on at different stops?

Questions for Further Reflection

1. How many on- and off-street parking spots does your church have?

2. How does your church view its parking spaces? Is your church more like the innkeeper in Luke 2, "there is no room in the inn"? Or is your church more like Jesus proclaiming abundance with only six loaves and two fish?

3. How many hours a day are the spaces occupied? How many days are they open?

4. What else could happen in your church parking lot (church plaza) besides parking? Kickball game? Labyrinth night? Could you host a farmers market? Artists bazaar? Food truck gathering? Bike obstacle course?

5. Do you know the names of the neighbors who border your church's property? Who are they? How long have they lived there? What do they think of the church?

6. How close is your church to a bus/light rail/streetcar route? How frequently does it run on a Sunday morning? Have you ever ridden public transit to church? Do you have transit schedules in your information rack at church?

7. Does your church have bike parking? How close is your church to a bike lane? Where is the nearest locally owned bike shop? Is there a minority-owned bike shop in your neighborhood or city? Go to a bike shop, introduce yourself, tell them you want to make your church more bike-friendly. Ask them if they could come to your church and give you some ideas.

8. What is your church's walk score? Walk Score is a private company that provides a "score" for how walkable a property is. How close to restaurants, schools, shopping, cultural activities, parks, etc. They also provide transit scores and bike scores. Judson's walk score is 68, transit score is 54, and bike score is 75. Scores can be obtained, free of charge, at www.walkscore.com. What can you do to improve it? How many people walk past your church on a Sunday morning? On a Tuesday afternoon? Ask volunteers to sit on a chair at the church and count passersby.

9. What apps does your city offer for public transit? Bike share? Do you have them downloaded to your phone?

10. How much does it cost to take public transit in your city? Where can you purchase prepaid fare cards? Who do you know that has a public transit fare card?

Suggested Reading List

Holmgren, David. *Retrosuburbia: The Downshifter's Guide to a Resilient Future*. Victoria, Australia: Melliodora Publishing, 2018. David Holmgren walks you through how to adopt permaculture practices for your suburban lifestyle with pictures, asides, charts, stories, and wisdom.

Shoup, Donald. *The High Cost of Free Parking*. Chicago: American Planning Association Planners Press, 2011. At 765 pages it may be more than you want to tackle, but it is worth it. You can also join the "Shoupistas" Facebook group and learn all you desire about parking. I would also suggest Carlton Reid's podcast from July 18, 2020, "In Conversation with the Rock Star of Parking, Donald Shoup" at https://www.the-spokesmen.com/donaldshoup/.

The Transition Network (https://transitionnetwork.org) started by Rob Hopkins in Dartington, England, in the early 2000s, is a resource for transitioning from oil dependency to local resilience. The website offers guides, workshops, and local transition groups near you.

Word and World: Theology for Christian Ministry Journal, Vol. 28, No. 3, Summer 2008, "The Automobile," https://wordandworld.luthersem.edu/issues.aspx?issue_id=111.

Forthcoming research by Dr. Laura Hartman, professor of Environmental Studies at Roanoke College. Dr. Hartman's recent research focuses on church parking lots, https://directory.roanoke.edu/faculty?username=hartman.

Straw Bale Gardening resources by Joel Kartsen. Visit https://strawbalegardens.com, where you can order his book (or check it out from your local library), view resources, watch his TED Talk, follow on Instagram, and join the Facebook discussion group.

Recipe: Church Plaza Pizza

Every summer, a colleague of mine, the Rev. Jane McBride of First Congregational Church in Minneapolis, hosts pizza night at her church. The congregation has a portable pizza oven (more about this in the next chapter) that they roll out in the summer and park in their small parking lot. The church makes dough ahead of time and provides sauce and cheese; congregants/neighbors supply their own toppings.

Here is my foolproof/time-tested pizza dough you can make at home or for your church plaza gathering.

3 cups all-purpose flour
1 tablespoon salt
1 teaspoon instant yeast (not active)
1 tablespoon olive oil
1 cup + 2 tablespoons water

Mix the dry ingredients in a bowl, then add the water and olive oil. You can mix the dough with your hand, with a wooden spoon, or with a stand mixer. Mix until blended well, then knead until dough is smooth and supple.

Maybe kneading dough is not a skill you have acquired; that is okay. Knead for five minutes. Coat the dough ball with oil, then cover and let rise in the refrigerator until the next afternoon.

Preheat your oven to at least 500 degrees. When it reaches 500, take the dough from the fridge, cut it into three sections and form each section into a ball. Cover with a towel and let rest for 30 minutes. Sprinkle some flour on your work surface and shape one of the dough balls into a pizza crust. You can gently pull it with your hands, you can roll it out with a rolling pin, or you can toss it in the air (if you've never done this before, you probably want to watch a YouTube video first). If the dough feels like it is fighting against you, let the gluten relax by leaving the dough alone for five minutes. Once you have acquired the perfect-size pizza crust, take some olive oil and brush around the edges of your crust, then sprinkle some kosher salt on the edge.

You've got two choices now. One, you can put your dough onto a floured pizza peel, or the back of a sheet pan, and top with sauce and toppings. Or, two, you can par-bake your crust for four or five minutes, then top your pizza. Why do this? It allows you some grace and prevents your pizza dough from sticking to the peel or toppings falling off when you place it in the oven.

Place sauce, cheese, and toppings on crust and bake for 5-7 minutes, watching closely for your preferred doneness.
Sauce: It will thicken as it cooks, so don't be afraid to add a couple of teaspoons or tablespoons of water to your sauce to thin it out before you spread it on.
Cheese: Try to include three varieties (mozzarella + one hard cheese like Parmesan) and a smoky Gouda or a few chunks of blue cheese.
Toppings: On one half, go for your tried and true toppings. On the other half, be experimental; try browned onions and red peppers and goat cheese or blue cheese and roasted beets or ham and Gruyere cheese.

NOTES

1. Eran Ben-Joseph, "From Chaos to Order: A Brief Cultural History of the Parking Lot," *The Mit Press Reader,* September 30, 2020, https://thereader.mitpress.mit.edu/brief-cultural-history-of-the-parking-lot/.

2. Harold Dean Trulear, "Conquering Space: Mister Rogers' Neighborhood." Living Pulpit 11, No. 3 (Jul–Sep 2002), 10.

3. John Rhodes, "Anabaptist Technology: Lessons from a Communitarian Business," *Plough* Quarterly, No. 15, January 8, 2018, https://www.plough.com/en/topics/faith/anabaptists/anabaptist-technology. This is a quote from Neil Postman's book *Technopoly: The Surrender of Culture to Technology* (New York: Vintage, 1993), 15.

4. Pamela Fickenscher and William Schroeer, personal interview. July 8, 2020. They provided the idea of a plaza.

5. Pamela Fickenscher and William Schroeer, "Actually, You Did Go to Seminary to Deal with Parking!" *Word and World*, vol. 28, no. 3, 2008, 250–251.

6. Ibid.

7. "The Bris." *Seinfeld*: Season Five written by Tom Cherones, directed by Larry Charles. NBC, season 5, episode 5, October 4, 1993.

8. Jana Schleis, "Making a Milwaukee Beach Accessible," Central Time, Wisconsin Public Radio, KUWS, Superior, August 12, 2020, https://www.wpr.org/listen/1681241. This was a term used on this program to remind the able-bodied, we are truly only temporarily able-bodied.

9. Mall Walking: A Program Resource Guide, Centers for Disease Control, https://www.cdc.gov/physicalactivity/downloads/mallwalking-guide.pdf.

10. Sophie Williams, "People in the US use car parking spaces for offices," *BBC News*, May 1, 2019, https://www.bbc.com/news/world-us-canada-48114878.

11. "The Park(ing) Day Manual," Rebar Group, https://www.asla.org/uploadedFiles/CMS/Events/Parking_Day_Manual_Consecutive.pdf.

12. To understand more of Gene Logsdon's unusual approach to farming, see his book, *Holy Shit: How to Manage Manure to Save Mankind* (Hartford, VT: Chelsea Green Publishing, 2010).

13. The image was made freely available to encourage walking, biking, and public transit. Urban Cycling, October 2, 2012, https://veloaficionado.com/blog/cycling-promotion-fund-canberra-transport-photo.

Chapter 3

Resources: Staff, Building, and Money

n the last chapter, I showed how you could transform parking lots into plazas, or if you are parking-poor, how you can transform your lack of parking into a blessing and not a curse. Now we are ready to introduce movement into your three other greatest resources: staff, building, and money. A divinity school professor once quipped, "If you want to know a church's theology, don't look at their belief statements but at their budget." If you look at almost any city-neighborhood church's budget, you will see two theological proclamations: the importance of people (staff) and the importance of place (building). The two questions to ask are: 1) What are the costs/implications of staff remaining mostly in the office? 2) What are the costs of using the building for members only?

Staff

One fine summer day during my first pastorate in Athens, West Virginia, I decided to walk around town for my afternoon visits. I walked down Vermillion Street and knocked on the door of a retired college professor Dr. Arthur Benson and his amazing life partner, Mrs. Irene Benson. Dr. Benson came to the door and welcomed me in. We had a nice visit that was made especially nice with a slice of pecan pie, a scoop of ice cream, and a cup of coffee. As I left, he walked me to the door and paused for a moment. He looked up the street and down the street with a quizzical look. Then he turned to me and asked, "Preacher, don't we pay you enough to drive a car for visits?" Rather than give him an honest answer, I asked if Mrs. Benson used light or dark brown sugar in her pecan pie. He took the bait and replied, "Neither. She uses molasses." I told him thanks and walked home.

I ducked Dr. Benson's question because the truth of the matter was that the church did not pay me enough to drive a car for visits. I thought I needed to own a car to be a pastor and the church thought I needed to own a car to be a pastor. The church and I both bought into the car-centered model of ministry as the common wisdom of the day. The church never considered the financial toll of car-centered ministry; more importantly, the church never considered the relational toll of a car-centered ministry.

To be fair to Athens Baptist Church, I do not know of any denomination that considers these tolls either. The only instance I have ever read is in the unprepared remarks Pope Francis gave in 2013 to six thousand future priests, brothers, and nuns. He revealed that "it pains him when he sees a nun or priest driving an expensive car, and he praised the beauty of the bicycle, noting his fifty-four-year-old personal secretary, Msgr. Alfred Xuereb, gets around on a bike."[1]

The Financial Costs of Car-Centric Ministry

Environmental author and activist Bill McKibben says, in his 2007 book *Deep Economy*: "Households can save as much as $750,000 over a lifetime if the bus system works well enough to enable people not to buy a second car."[2]

In 2019, AAA reported that the average cost per year, per vehicle, of a new automobile, was $9,282.35.[3] If you own a small sedan, the cheapest per-year vehicle, your automobile costs per year are still $3,483 (fuel and maintenance $1,689, insurance and registration fees $1,794).[4] Compare yearly costs of operating a sedan, $3,483, to the yearly costs for public transit in

America's most expensive public transit city, New York, $1,524. Or compare the yearly costs of operating a sedan, $3,483, to every year purchasing a new, fully equipped (fenders, lights, and bags) commuting bike, $700. That's $3,843 a year to pay down debt, or $3,843 to pay off student loans, or $3,843 to place in a savings account. Think of the public witness churches could have by sharing this wisdom with their members, community, and neighborhood. Churches could challenge the dominant paradigm of two-plus vehicles per family and the need for new (and heavier and more dangerous) vehicles by encouraging congregants to eliminate one car and take public transit, bicycle, and walk more often.

Furthermore, is it a sound financial practice to invest $20,000 (the average price of a 2020 small sedan)[5] on an object that remains unused 95 percent of the time,[6] depreciates yearly, and costs so much to operate and maintain?

Adam Ozimek, chief economist at Upwork, posted on Twitter: "Spending $40,000 on a car seems like the kind of thing to me that, intuitively, you do when you have like a couple million in wealth and make $400,000 a year. But absolutely normal people do it all the time! Blows me away."[7] (Note the average price for a new vehicle in 2019 in the United States was $36,718[8] with an APR interest rate of 6.28 percent and loan terms going beyond seven years.) This seemingly innocent tweet, which states obvious economic wisdom, brought out the vile replies one would expect from a political debate. People took his tweet personally— too personally. He was offering an alternative way to live a healthy economic life, and people attacked him.

The Relational Costs of Car-Centric Ministry

Consider for the moment how relying solely on a car for transit or ministry prevents you from engaging with your community. The day-to-day movement of the church mirrors the movement of the vast majority of Americans: protected (in a car) and alone (in a car). Inside these "sanctuaries of steel exoskeletons," we reinforce our cultural bubbles by listening to NPR or talk radio or podcasts or music or audiobooks, or talking to friends, or doing work, or re-securing our loneliness. But what if this mode of movement is part of the problem of church stagnation? What is the social or community cost of this type of movement?

Studies show that once drivers (and passengers) are traveling above 15 mph, they lose the ability to properly recognize faces.[9] Driving also demands tunnel vision in order to make the snap decisions necessary for navigation. These two factors change not only the way we see people but also how we judge people. Driving makes us more suspicious because we move too fast to fully see the other person. "Cars do their very best with their micro-controlled climates, audio, and even scents to seal the driver away from the rest of humanity (and from the impacts they themselves have on the environment: noise, fumes, and particulates) inside an aluminum box."[10]

However, when we walk, bicycle, and travel on public transit, we become more hopeful and more trusting of others because we engage with them face-to-face and see them at a "human speed." Also, the more we see one another face-to-face and engage one another at a human speed, we tend to trust more. These kinds of experiences release a surge of oxytocin, the "trust hormone."[11] When people experience a surge of oxytocin, they are more trusting, more empathetic, and more compassionate. Driving, especially driving alone, prevents us from having the kinds of experiences that nurture and deepen trust in our neighbors.

In 2007 the Vatican released *Guidelines for the Pastoral Care of the Road*; it is a thirty-six-page, four-part document. In section II, "Human Aspects," the authors describe how driving changes the driver. "When driving a vehicle, special circumstances may lead us to behave in an unsatisfactory and even barely human manner."[12] For a variety of reasons, driving a car makes us relive the apostle Paul's conundrum in Romans 7:19-20, KJV: "For the good that I would I do not: but the evil which I would not, that I do. Now if I do that I would not, it is no more I that do it, but sin that dwelleth in me."

To combat the inner workings and psychological effects of driving automobiles, the authors call for an additional skill to practice while driving: prayer. "During a journey it is also beneficial to pray vocally, especially taking turns with our fellow travelers in reciting the prayers, as when reciting the Rosary which, due to its rhythm and gentle repetition, does not distract the driver's attention. This will help to feel immersed in the presence of God, to stay under his protection, and may also give rise to a desire for communal or liturgical celebration, if possible at 'spiritually strategic' points along the road or railway (shrines, churches and chapels, including mobile ones)."[13]

Pause for a moment and consider the paragraph you just read: Driving a car changes the driver so much that you need to pray to keep your heart, mind, body, and soul intact while undertaking the task of driving! To see the animated truth of the Vatican document, go to YouTube and watch the 1950s Disney cartoon "Motor Mania." It is a Jekyll and Hyde story starring Goofy, who is calm, pleasant, and friendly when he walks (Mr. Walker), but when he gets behind the wheel of a car, he transforms into a horn-blaring, shouting, reckless driver (Mr. Wheeler).

I know what you are thinking: Don't let a few bad drivers ruin the rest of us who are conscientious and trusting souls. I believe you. Despite this, take a moment to reflect on how driving has affected the way you interact with your neighborhood and world.

- What are the names of five people in the neighborhood(s) between your home and your church? When did you last take a meal to someone in your neighborhood?
- From where you are reading this, point north. What phase is the moon currently in?
- What weather pattern does the direction of the wind foretell?
- When was the last time you shared space with someone who is not of the same race as you? Or not of the same socio-economic background as you? Or did not speak the same language as you?

For many people, driving a car is not a choice but rather a necessity. Many people live in areas where sidewalks are neither maintained nor adequate for wheelchair operation. Many people live in areas where transit service is neither available nor reliable nor accessible. Many people live in areas where bicycling is neither encouraged nor welcomed. In many cases, people are forced to drive because of infrastructure priorities, public policies, and private interests that are beyond the control of the driver. But there are ways people of faith can challenge those structures to make the world more loving, just, and flourishing.

The Reverend Walkers:
Tom Goldston and Biscuit Bill

The Rev. Tom Goldston was my predecessor at Athens Baptist Church by thirty years. He retired from pastoral ministry and settled in Athens shortly after I arrived. After retirement he was diagnosed with a heart condition that required him to walk for two hours every day. Athens was a small college town (population 400 without students, 1,600 with students) with sidewalks to the town limits. This meant Rev. Goldston had to walk several laps of the town and the college to get in his required exercise.

Rev. Goldston was a people person, so as he walked, he naturally waved at every car, truck, tractor, pedestrian, or bicyclist. Within days every car, truck, tractor, pedestrian, and bicyclist was waving or honking back at Tom. As I sat in my office, I knew instantly whether my window was open or not when Tom was nearby because of the commotion on the street. Everyone in town (and outside of town) knew Rev. Goldston as the man on the street who waved at everybody, but they did not know his name, whereas everyone in town (and out of town) knew my name: It was prominently displayed on the sign in front of the church. But no one (save for the few members at the church) knew who I was.

One day, out of boredom (and loneliness), I started walking around town and waving at everybody, just like Rev. Goldston did. Within a few weeks, I couldn't believe the transformation. I discovered a Catholic student house, an empty lot where the college's assistant men's basketball coach planted a vegetable garden, and a tiny food co-op that was only open once a week. More than those discoveries, walking the town nudged me to start meeting college students for coffee on campus rather than waiting for them to come to church on Sundays. Since I was on campus every few days, a biology professor invited me to play basketball with the faculty on Tuesdays and Thursdays. The more I was out of the office and walking the community, the more people began to know me and trust the church. Slowly, new people began showing up on Sunday mornings. It wasn't waves of new people, maybe one or two a Sunday, but you could feel the church changing.

Another walking reverend was Bill Bryce. Upon retiring from ministry, Bill started walking around Lake Harriet in south Minneapolis every morning. After a few mornings, he noticed the number of people walking dogs. One morning he put a few dog biscuits in his pocket to give away. Over time he began to build relationships, first with the dogs, then with their owners. Over time he went from the retired man nobody knew to the man with the dog biscuits to "Biscuit Bill." Over time, people asked Biscuit Bill if he would walk with them (and their dogs). As they walked, they began to trust one another and shared parts of their lives. When Biscuit Bill died, his walking friends shared at his funeral how Bill opened up about his experiences in World War II, his participation in the Freedom Summer campaign of 1964, and his time working with people who were incarcerated.

The walking revs, relieved of the pressure of building a church or keeping a ministry alive, were freed to do what they were created to do: interact in an authentic manner with God's creation. I look at their way of being present in retirement as a model of how pastors and church leaders can move out into the community: Initiate the hello, bring treats, and let the natural rhythm of walking move into friendship.

The Walking Evangelist

On June 2, 2020, Terry Willis started walking the 1,000-mile journey from his home in Huntsville, Alabama, to the site where George Floyd was killed in Minneapolis. Along the way he made stops in Louisville, Kentucky; Ferguson, Missouri; and Chicago to honor black victims killed by the police. Mr. Willis' silent protest march echoes the great witness of social justice marches in America: The Civil Rights Movement marches of the 1950s and '60s, the Native American marches such as the "Trail of Tears" in 1972, and "The Long Walk for Survival" in 1980, which inspired the Great Peace March for Global Nuclear Disarmament in 1986, which inspired the Great March for Climate Action in 2013.

These long and slow walks brought awareness of issues, passions for justice, and pleas for change. When Terry Willis walked by my house, it was like watching a living saint walking in my city. Hundreds of people lined Chicago Avenue to cheer and greet and encourage the young man from Alabama. As he walked by me, he looked exhausted and weak, but at the same time he looked like the strongest human being I had ever seen. He was sobbing, overcome by emotion. His only words were "Bless you" and "I love you." When he arrived at 38th Street and Chicago Avenue, he took off his shoes and left them at the site of George Floyd's killing. He addressed the crowd with an exhausted voice. Listeners had to concentrate on every word. His message was simple: Change, love, and let's build the beloved community together. These marches are part of a tradition of American walks for social justice. Perhaps the first was walked by John Woolman (1720–1772) of the American Society of Friends (Quakers). Woolman was a clerk in Mount Holly, New Jersey, when in 1742 a shopkeeper asked him to write a bill of sale for an enslaved woman. He wrote the bill of sale but felt afflicted. The affliction in his soul continued and manifested as a resolve within the Quaker tradition to end the practice of enslaving human beings.

Woolman expressed this by walking up and down the eastern coast of the British colonies (he also sailed to Barbados and to

England, where he died). In March 1766 he announced his intentions to visit with Friends in the lower counties of Pennsylvania and the Maryland coast.

His approach was simple: "To travel on foot among them (Friends) that by so travelling I might have a livelier feeling of the condition of the oppressed slaves, set an example of lowliness before the eyes of their masters, and be more out of the way of temptation to unprofitable converse."[14] His goal was to talk with Friends who enslaved human beings and talk them out of the practice. During his lifetime, sometimes he was successful, sometimes he was not. Nevertheless, because of his efforts, by the end of the American Revolution, no Friends engaged in the practice of selling or owning people.

For a moment, contrast the actions of John Woolman and George Whitfield, another traveling religious figure in the British colonies. Whitfield is widely credited with starting the First Great Awakening, a time of religious revival in the colonies. He came to America with passions for both anti-slavery sentiments and religious conversion, but only one of those passions made it into his preaching efforts. The First Great Awakening chose to exclude abolition. Woolman, however, started the tradition within American Christianity that one can both advocate for social justice and experience religious renewal. His pattern also illustrates how social change can happen: methodically and personally. Many times, faith leaders call for change without knowing exactly what they are asking for, or who they are calling to change. Woolman knew whom he needed to address: Friends who enslaved human beings. He walked hundreds of miles to the Carolinas and back to New Jersey, he knocked on doors, he had conversations, he ate with them, he stayed the night in their homes, he prayed, he poured his heart out, and he asked them to change.

The Building

On the evening of April 15, 2019, a fire broke out in the Catholic cathedral of Notre-Dame de Paris. Fifteen hours later, the cathedral's roof and spire had been consumed. Parisians and lovers of the cathedral worldwide immediately pledged $880 million toward the rebuilding. I doubt the world knows your church building or what it looks, smells, feels, sounds, or tastes like. But it is safe to say your church building acts, for your community, as its own "Our Lady of Paris." If your walls and pews could talk, they would tell uplifting and heartbreaking stories of weddings and funerals. They would tell stories of kids doing mischievous deeds and adults gossiping after worship services. They would tell stories of suppers and bake sales and lock-ins and roof leaks and boiler replacements and stewardship campaigns. Our buildings are amazing assets, but sometimes they can feel like a drain of resources and time and energy.[15]

Do you view your building as a liability or an asset for ministry? Does your building enhance or inhibit your ministry?

Some people think churches should not own buildings; they think the monies used for maintaining them should be used for other purposes. If you ask what other purposes, critics often respond that the money should be used for feeding the hungry or housing those experiencing homelessness or for healing the community or peace efforts, etc. Those are just and proper criticisms of funds being used on a building when they could be invested in people and relationships and communities in need. What if the building was more than a drain of resources? What if it was a generator of resources? What if it was a place of meeting, a place of healing, a place of joy?

When small city-neighborhood churches lose their neighborhood connection, they lose both their pastoral presence (a place for the community to pause, reflect, and heal) and their prophetic power (a place to dream, challenge, and repent). Churches (and church buildings) bereft of pastoral and prophetic power then become the target, and rightly so, of calls for using funds spent on the building to be used elsewhere.

One church in Los Angeles sold its building but kept its parking lot. On Sunday mornings they set up several tents and have worship, then lease out the 100 spots to commuters and concertgoers the rest of the week. This may not work in some parts of North America, but it is working for the Reverend Mandy McDow and the congregation of Los Angeles First United Methodist Church.

Moving into the Parish with Your Building

The challenge/opportunity is to align your ministry with your building. How can your church both, simultaneously, move into the community with your building and invite your community to your building? In 2014, Sara Joy Proppe founded the Proximity Project, with a mission to "empower churches to connect their mission and their story to their physical place in the neighborhood."[16] Her work has made me realize the importance of the outside of the building and how people interact with it.

One place to start is with an audit of your church building. To do this, I suggest you invite someone who neither goes to your church nor is part of a faith community at all. Let fresh eyes reveal to you the abundance of your facilities. You will find that an outsider will have a deeper appreciation of your building than you will. What does your building offer that the community does not have?

Here is a small list to help you get started:

- High ceilings
- An acoustic environment built for a piano, an organ, a violin, a chamber orchestra, a choir, a jazz combo, a bluegrass pickin' parlor, a child's recital, a local play, etc.
- Space to roam and play, pews to crawl under
- Library full of books, most of which cannot be found at public libraries
- Kitchen (probably industrial) with large pots and pans and coffee urns
- Sunday School rooms
- Office space

- Roofs that soak up the sun's rays
- Playground (maybe)
- Parking lot/plaza with a basketball court (maybe)
- Greenspace

Some churches bake their own communion bread. What if you grew your own wheat and made your own flour to bake your own communion bread in your parking plaza or green space? In the early 2010s the Environmental Youth Alliance in Vancouver, British Columbia, began a new experiment: Lawns to Loaves. They asked people throughout the city to forgo growing grass (North America's largest monocrop) and grow wheat instead. Around the city, owners of twenty small lots participated in this initiative, and in the fall the wheat was harvested, threshed, ground into flour, kneaded into pizza dough, then baked on outdoor pizza ovens. What does this have to do with churches? Churches too could forgo growing grass and plant wheat—they could even grow wheat in a parking space! And what if you had an outdoor oven to bake the bread? When Our Savior Lutheran Church and Holy Trinity Lutheran Church, both in Minneapolis, reimagined their limited outdoor green space, they both built outdoor hearth/pizza ovens for the community to use.

Do not neglect the opportunity city-neighborhood churches have over suburban and exurban megachurches: foot traffic. When you drive past a building at thirty-five or fifty-five miles an hour, you do not have a chance to fully grasp it, but when you mosey by on an evening stroll or while taking your dog for a walk you have an opportunity to take a building in. Don't neglect the boring church sign or the efficacy of sandwich boards to communicate, or the impact of a simple banner. These are invaluable tools to communicate with your outside voice who your church is on the inside.

While in New Orleans I once preached a sermon series on the Seven Deadly Sins. For less than $100, a banner was made that hung along the sidewalk. The banner announced the sermon series with a giant "7" surrounded by the sins: lust, gluttony, greed, sloth, wrath, envy, and pride. To my surprise the banner became a selfie hotspot. All during Lent that year, my phone didn't stop dinging because every time someone took a picture, tagged the church, and shared it on social media, my phone alerted me. There was no way we could have bought that kind of publicity for $100!

Urban and city-neighborhood churches may not have the unlimited acreage of suburban congregations, but they can maximize their space in ways suburban congregations cannot. Judson Church is trying to maximize every square inch of its outdoor space. We have a playground for our preschool that the community uses, a Little Free Library, a peace pole designed and decorated by the youth, a rain garden with native plants, and ample bike parking. But we know we can do more. The Rev. Michael Piazza, in his work as a church consultant, once had a church place a chalkboard beside the sidewalk with a piece of chalk tied to it and wrote on the top, for passersby to complete, this sentence, "Before I die . . ." At another church he advised leaders to purchase and hang gigantic rainbow flags from their building to announce, unequivocally, their support for the LGBTQIA+ community.[17] I would also suggest you conduct an audit of what is missing. At Judson Church we need a bench to encourage contemplation and rest, we need a prayer wall to give people a place to grieve, lament, or praise, and we need to make our newsletter available and more accessible to our neighbors.

Several years ago, I heard the Rev. J. Bennett Guess, then a United Church of Christ national staff member, say that "churches must keep constant, the drumbeat of invitation open to the community." It takes time for neighbors and the neighborhood to see that who you say you are matches your actions, or who you say you are matches your actions, or your outside voice matches your inside voice. Having this in mind, I ask: Does our building invite people to explore what we do? Does it express our values and concerns? Does it communicate the gospel?

Inviting the Parish into the Building

When Calvary Church in Minneapolis updated their fellowship hall kitchen, they did so with the intent of having community members use it. They also rent it. Several startup baking and cooking companies rent the industrial kitchen. When University Baptist Church in Minneapolis updated their fellowship hall, they did so with the intent of hosting live music. Nearly every weekend, UBC hosts grassroots and folk music concerts.

One of the goals of Judson Church is to have the building in use as much as possible. Within the last year, we have had an opera company, a jazz combo, a trombone choir, and a blues band use our sanctuary as practice space. On most days, a local jazz pianist is practicing on our baby grand or a local organ professor is practicing on our pipe organ. We have been the host site for the Martin Luther King Jr. Community Breakfast, and we have hosted community conversations led by our city of Minneapolis councilmember. In addition to regular Judson worship services, meetings, and classes, the church also houses the Judson Preschool and Meals on Wheels, and we are the home of four licensed counselors, a neighborhood association, offices for a philharmonic orchestra, two Girl Scout troops, a watercolor painting group, and a women's strength training class (Women with Balls). But no one is using our kitchen. We have yet to open our library for the community to browse and borrow or use as a reading room. We are exploring how to open our sanctuary for the community to enjoy in silence, light a prayer candle, or listen to a noontime piano or organ or jazz concert. Our building is an asset to our ministry.

Money

The Economics of Jesus

Historians refer to the 207 years between 27 BCE and 180 CE as the Pax Romana, or the Peace of Rome. If you were a member of the elite living luxuriously on the banks of the River Tiber, I am sure it was peaceful. If, however, you lived under Roman occupation, it was anything but peaceful. It was more like Vexatio Romana, or the Violent Oppression or "Hell" of Rome. Villagers throughout Israel resented their occupiers but were faced with only two options: Resist and die, or capitulate and rot from the inside out. In this world Jesus walked, taught, healed, told stories, and offered a third way.

Jesus' third way is most clear and visible and present in his teachings, healings, actions, and stories. The third way is particularly clear in the stories he told; in his stories he offered a way where villagers could live with integrity, nurture their relationships, and expand their love. The way offered was an alternative lifestyle, rooted in the ancient Israelite traditions of hospitality, healing, and prophetic actions, a way that went counter to the dominant policies and practices of Roman occupation. We can see the effects of Roman policies by reading and hearing Jesus' parables backward, reading them slowly, questioning why Jesus is telling the story the way he is.

Grab your Bible and read Luke 11:5-8 in this light. A friend knocks on your door at midnight, asking for three loaves of bread because your friend is out and needs to offer hospitality to a stranger. What do you do? Do you turn your friend away because you are fearful of opening your door at such a late hour? Do you tell your friend to go away because you do not have three loaves to spare because you have to feed your family? The dilemma symbolizes the choices Jesus' audience faced. Do they practice hospitality and risk vulnerability? Do they turn away a friend in need? Do they lean into a new way of being or do they shut the door?

Reading the parable with these questions in our minds, we can picture a people who were distrustful of outsiders, reluctant to help the wounded, hesitant to share, and scared to visit those in prisons. In his stories, Jesus revealed to the audience that they could reclaim and revive their ancient practices. Viewed in this light, Jesus' stories/parables become not earthly stories with heavenly meanings, but earthly stories with heavy (here and now) meanings.

The Knock at Midnight

After George Floyd was killed by four Minneapolis police officers on May 25, 2020, I heard members of the police force, politicians, the business community, education systems, and social work organizations all express a form of repentance. I heard many words and thoughts and prayers for reconciliation. But I heard few, if any, words concerning economic reparations. Many church-goers throughout the Twin Cities followed a well-worn pattern: They formed book groups and committees and task forces centered on racial justice. Many were out on the street marching and protesting. These actions, both admirable and necessary, repeated a cycle I have watched take place again and again over my lifetime. These actions never seem to break the grip of systemic racism.

The killing of Floyd and the unrest afterward impacted the Judson community and the Twin Cities. For a week my front yard was littered with chunks of debris from the buildings that had burned the night before. Someone spray-painted the church and tried to start a fire on our front doors. As a church we had to ask ourselves: We hear the knock at midnight, so how will we respond? We knew we couldn't keep doing the same thing over and over. Yes, we have formed reading groups. Yes, we have formed task forces. Yes, we are seeking new relationships within the black community. But we are also trying one new effort: initiating economic reparations.[18] Reparations are a way for us to use our resources of money to move into the community and establish new relationships.

Introducing the idea of reparations needs to be done with calm courage. You will encounter a chorus of scarcity: "There isn't enough to go around." "Where would we even start?" "Would our small contribution even matter?" Let us take these objections point by point.

There isn't enough to go around: When the pandemic first started, the Judson Church council started a community fund to help members who had lost their jobs or experienced financial hardship because of COVID-19. We raised $10,000 in a week.

After the uprisings, we expanded this fund to include helping our community. In a week, we raised $35,000. In the midst of a pandemic, in the midst of high unemployment, in the midst of not knowing what tomorrow would bring, a small city-neighborhood church raised $50,000 over and beyond its budget.

Where would we even start? The entire journey of this book thus far and onward is about how faith communities can share space and connect and form relationships with those with their backs against the wall. You start with those you know or close by and listen and take notes. You repent and tenderize your heart.

Would our small contribution even matter? To this I say, regardless of size, it would be more than you ever did before!

A cautionary note: Take your time for this endeavor. Judson Church is fortunate to be in relationship with two black leaders in Minneapolis: Don and Sondra Samuels. Don is an ordained Baptist minister who was also a member of the Minneapolis City Council and School Board; he is now the CEO of Microgrants, a micro-lending nonprofit in North Minneapolis. Sondra is the president and CEO of the Northside Achievement Zone, modeled after the Harlem Children's Zone in New York City. When I asked Don and Sondra for their reaction to white churches starting reparations funds, they paused before answering. Don took a deep breath and said, "I'm glad you are using that word, reparations. Because it means you are seeking to repair a relationship." They went on to encourage white churches to take a contemplative approach to the formation of a reparations fund. "Before you act, incorporate silence into meetings and worship. Why not invite silence, and in that silence, seek the will of God in your quest for reparations and for this fund."[19]

When we move out into the community with our resources (staff, building, and money), we invite the community into our building. When our staff is out in the community, when our buildings use their outside voices to reveal our inside values, when our funds are used in a way to start new relationships, change will happen, hearts will soften, and renewal will take place. But it takes time, the topic of the next chapter . . .

Prayer

In the spirit of the song *People in Your Neighborhood* from Sesame Street:

> *Living God, Oh, who are the people in my neighborhood? In my neighborhood?*
> *In my neighborhood?*
> *Say God, who are the people in my neighborhood? The people I need to meet each day*
> *Amen.*

Experiment: Create A BIPOC (Black, Indigenous, and People of Color) Business Directory

During a panel discussion at the 2016 New Baptist Covenant meeting, someone from the crowd asked Rev. Dr. Kevin Cosby (pastor of St. Stephen Baptist Church and president of Simmons College in Louisville, Kentucky) what would be the most significant actions a white church could take for racial justice. Rev. Cosby instantly responded, "Act with your wallet!" He went on to describe a situation I have heard and been a part of many times: A white church wants to wade into the waters of racial justice and they start reading books, they form working groups, they make statements, they sing spirituals, but when it comes time to put on a new roof, or cater a meal, or purchase a new banner, white churches usually stick with the relationships they know best: white-owned businesses. Rev. Cosby drove home the point that in order to break this cycle and enter into new relationships with the black community, white churches have to intentionally seek and discover and invest in black-owned businesses.

The conversation continued when the Rev. Joe Phelps, who shared the panel with Rev. Cosby, told the story of Stokely's List, a black-owned business directory. Members of Crescent Hill Baptist Church in Louisville compiled the list from information the black community provided after realizing they did not know where to start looking for black-owned businesses.[20] When I talked with the pastor of Crescent Hill Baptist Church, the Rev.

Jason Crosby, he told me the ways individuals from the congregation, and the congregation as an institution have used the list. The list has provided a way for the church to enter into new relationships with the black community of Louisville. Compiling the list has also exposed the deeper ways systemic racism works in our society. Specifically, most of the businesses on the list are mom-and-pop and small, family-owned businesses: funeral homes, realtors, restaurants, barber and beauty shops, small construction contractors. Where are the large-scale businesses, paper supply companies, HVAC contractors, concrete companies? Form a task force or ad hoc committee with the sole purpose of compiling a list of BIPOC-owned businesses in your community.

Questions for Further Reflection

1. How much do you spend per month on automobile ownership? Include gas, insurance, registration fees, and maintenance.

2. How much does it cost for a monthly public transit card? At your church, are there any displays how public transit works? Public transit maps and schedules?

3. Does your church engage with any BIPOC-owned businesses? If so, how did the arrangements come about? Recommendations? Word of mouth? Advertisements? If your church does not engage with BIPOC-owned businesses, why not? Has the topic ever been a subject at a church meeting?

4. Read two stories in Luke (the story of the rich young ruler, 18:18-30, and the story of Zacchaeus, 19:1-10). One is asked to sell everything, and the other gives half away and promises to pay four-fold to make up for those he defrauded. How can your church become more like Zacchaeus and less like the rich young ruler?

5. How many BIPOC-owned businesses are in your "parish"?

6. Does your church have a section dedicated to giving on its website? Do you include links to a BIPOC-owned business directory on that page? If not, could you? How much of your church budget goes toward Zacchaeus-type ministries: repentance, reconciliation, reparations?

7. Describe a situation where your small sacrifice enabled someone else to experience joy.

8. If you had an extra $3,000 a year, what would you spend it on?

9. Who is in your circle of influence? Make a list of neighbors, co-workers, acquaintances, club members of people who are influencers, managers, business owners, CEOs, etc. How could you approach them to join you in patronizing BIPOC-owned businesses? How could you talk with them about generosity? Supporting and giving to the common good?

10. How much of your personal or family budget goes toward Zacchaeus-type ministries: repentance, reconciliation, reparations?

Suggested Reading List

Blue, Elly. *Bikenomics: How Bicycling Can Save the Economy* (Portland: Microsom, 2016). This book reveals how bicycling and going car-free or car-lite is good for both individuals and businesses.

Evans, Joseph. *Reconciliation and Reparations: Preaching Economic Justice* (Valley Forge, PA: Judson, 2018). Dean of the Morehouse School of Religion, Dr. Evans provides sermons and prophetic essays on Christian economic/racial justice.

Herzog, William R. *Parables as Subversive Speech: Jesus and the Pedagogy of the Oppressed* (Louisville, KY: Westminster/John Knox, 1994). Dr. Herzog's groundbreaking work on the parables.

Juster, Norton, author, illustrated by Raschka, Chris. *The Hello, Goodbye Window* (San Francisco: Hyperion, 2006). A good primer on how to begin and end relationships.

Klein, Naomi. *This Changes Everything: Capitalism vs. The Climate* (New York: Simon and Schuster, 2014). The title says it all.

Rogers, Fred. *The Giving Box: Create a Tradition of Giving with Your Children* (Philadelphia, PA: Running, 2000). A wonderful book of stories about the importance of giving (this is more than a really good children's book; it's a great book for everyone).

Tatenhove, Krin Van and Mueller, Rob. *Neighborhood Church: Transforming Your Congregation into a Powerhouse for Mission* (Louisville KY: Westminster/John Knox, 2019). This book applies ABCD (asset-based community development) principles to the local church.

Thistlethwaite, Susan. *#Occupy the Bible: What Jesus Really Said (And Did) About Money And Power* (New York: Astor + Blue Editions, 2014). Dr. Thistlethwaite's writing is clear, concise, and poignant as she looks at the implications of the Occupy Wall Street movement and the teachings of Jesus.

Any books, articles, lectures, or classes by the Rev. Donna Schaper, senior pastor of Judson Memorial Church in New York, New York. She has a creative and generous spirit for finding ways for small but mighty churches to thrive.

Recipe: Instant Pot Pulled Pork BBQ

Several years ago, I heard a story on NPR about the Instant Pot, an electric pressure cooker. I was intrigued by the machine and did some investigating. When I revealed my findings to Lori, she was quite enthralled with the sauté function. She remarked, "This is genius; this saves cleaning up another pan!" So, we bought one, and we couldn't be happier with it. We use it to cook dried beans, chicken, and pot roast. It is great for chicken, beef, or vegetable stock. I cook beets any chance I get (with my daughter away at college, I'm the only one who loves beets). But the greatest gift of this kitchen tool is time. Lori and I can prep dinner, put it in the Instant Pot (or Magic Pot, as Lori calls it), and then go about our evening to continue work or do laundry or enjoy happy hour together.

I love to cook Pulled Pork BBQ. I love to cook it all day on a Saturday over a grill, via indirect heat, and enjoy the aroma. But I also love to work in the garden, enjoy time with my kids and friends, go for bike rides, and go to the farmers markets on Saturdays. Yes, this is "cheating," but it's good cheating.

You'll need a pork shoulder with a shoulder blade. Most grocery stores sell two- to three-pound pork shoulders. This recipe is for a three-pound shoulder. I prefer one pound per person, as this gives you a satisfying meal and plenty of leftovers for pulled pork tacos or pulled pork pizza.

The night before you want to serve the pulled pork, make the spice mix and rinse the shoulder with water, pat dry, and place on sheet pan.

In a mixing bowl, combine:

½ cup brown sugar
½ cup salt
1 tablespoon garlic powder
1 tablespoon chipotle powder
1 tablespoon cumin
1 tablespoon curry powder
1 tablespoon fresh ground pepper
1 tablespoon smoked paprika

Stir together, then pour liberally over the pork shoulder. Cover shoulder with plastic wrap and place in fridge.

Three hours before dinner, remove plastic wrap. Push the sauté button on your Instant Pot. Note: Some people wash off the spice rub before cooking the pork, but I like to leave it on.

Sear pork on all sides, about 3–4 minutes per side. Place one can of beer or one cup of water in the pot with the pork. Cover and set to cook for 90 minutes. When cooking is complete, release pressure and turn on the oven broiler. Place pork on a clean sheet pan. Break up the pork into chunks; it will be so tender it will fall apart easily. Place under the broiler until the top layer crisps up.

Remove and let rest.

If you have a gravy separator, pour the liquid from the Instant Pot into the separator to separate the fat. If you do not have a gravy separator, fill a large bowl with ice water. Pour the liquid from the Instant Pot into a small bowl. Place the small bowl into the large bowl and put into the freezer for one hour. After an hour, skim off the fat. Pour the "fat-free" liquid back into the pot and sauté, reducing by at least half. Add ¼ cup of apple cider vinegar and a teaspoon of red pepper flakes and bring to a boil. Turn off pot.

Place pulled pork on pretzel buns and pour some of the sauce onto it. Enjoy with fries, chips, baked beans, or sweet potato fries or even without the buns over rice.

NOTES

1. Carol Glatz, "Avoid fast cars and ride a bike instead, Pope tells trainee priests and nuns," *Catholic Herald*, July 9, 2013, https://catholicherald.co.uk/avoid-fast-cars-and-ride-a-bike-instead-pope-tells-trainee-priests/.

2. Bill McKibben, *Deep Economy: The Wealth of Communities and the Durable Future* (New York: Times Books, 2007), 154.

3. Figures compiled from Your Driving Costs: How Much Are You Really Paying to Drive? AAA Association Communication, https://exchange.aaa.com/wp-content/uploads/2019/09/AAA-Your-Driving-Costs-2019.pdf, They do not include depreciation and finance charges.

4. Ibid.

5. Kelly Blue Book Editors, "2020 New Car Buyer's Guide," May 14, 2020, https://www.kbb.com/car-news/new-car-and-suv-buyers-guides/.

6. David Z. Morris, "Today's Cars Are Parked 95 percent of the Time," Fortune.com, March 13, 2016, https://fortune.com/2016/03/13/cars-parked-95- percent-of-time/.

7. Adam Ozimek (@ModeledBehavior), 2:24 Sept. 7, 2020, Twitter.com, https://twitter.com/modeledbehavior/status/1303051417897390090.

8. Tailia James, "New Vehicle Prices Climb to Highest Level of the Year in April, According to Edmunds Analysis," May 1, 2019, Edmunds.com, https://www.edmunds.com/industry/press/new-vehicle-prices-climb-to-highest-level-of-the-year- in-april-according-to-edmunds-analysis.html.

9. The slowest average driving speed in the US is Boston's, at 17.6 mph, http://cityspeed.sourceforge.net.

10. Samuel I. Schwartz with William Rosen, *Street Smart: The Fall of Cars and the Rise of Cities* (New York: Public Affairs, 2015), 98.

11. Ibid., 99.

12. Renato Raffaele Cardinal Martino, II. 24 "Guidelines for the Pastoral Care of the Road," Section II, #24 People on the Move, August 2007.

13. Ibid., Section III, #60.

14. John Woolman, *The Journal of John Woolman and A Plea for the Poor* (New York: Citadel, 1961), 165.

15. Krin Van Tatenhove and Rob Mueller, *Neighborhood Church: Transforming Your Congregation into a Powerhouse for Mission* (Louisville, KY: Westminster John Knox Press, 2019),

76. "...second only to the gifts of our members, our physical buildings are the greatest assets at our disposal."

16. See https://www.proximityprojectinc.com/.

17. See https://www.agilechurch.com/.

18. Michael Eric Dyson, *Tears We Cannot Stop: A Sermon to White America* (New York: St. Martin's, 2017). At the end of the book, Dyson lists several practical and transformative actions white Christians can do now. One is the formation of IRAs: Individual Reparations Accounts.

19. Don and Sondra Samuels, personal interview, August 18, 2020.

20. Rev. Jason Crosby, personal conversation, December 4, 2020.

Chapter 9
Time

O ne of the limitations city-neighborhood pastors and church leaders face is time; either time is not on their side (the "time" to start a renewal program has passed) or there are not enough hours in the day or week to do all of the things that need to be done. There simply isn't enough time to do visits, prepare worship services, write sermons, go to meetings, and keep the church running **and** engage in church renewal initiatives and projects **and** be present in the community **and** be active at social justice rallies, marches, meetings, and gatherings **and** attend to your heart, mind, body, and soul. Something's gotta give.

I could tell that since walking, biking, and taking public transit, my concept of time and speed was transforming. I discovered these slow movements, ironically, created more time. These forms of transit are not efficient from a time perspective; driving a car is faster (sometimes). But as we saw in the last chapter, what you lose in speed, you gain in relationships. A similar phenomenon applies to time: The slower you go, the deeper the relationship and the more time is freed up.

Embracing Slow Church

In the midst of high-speed everything, a reactionary appreciation of slowness has arisen: slow food, slow money, slow medicine, Daniel Kahneman's book *Thinking Fast and Thinking Slow*, and Malcolm Gladwell's 10,000 hours rule. Authors C. Christopher Smith and John Pattison in 2014 offered *Slow Church: Cultivating*

Community in the Patient Way of Jesus. Their book emphasizes the time it takes to form and shape a community.[1]

The idea of a slow church/slow faith community is nothing new; in fact, it may be as old as the nation of Israel. Scholar (and extraordinary preacher) Ellen Davis, professor of Bible and Practical Theology at Duke Divinity School, offers the idea of Israel as an original slow community in her book *Scripture, Culture, and Agriculture: An Agrarian Reading of the Bible.* Israel was a spit of land with the sea on one side and the Fertile Crescent on the other. It was not a land flowing with milk and honey, but a land of rocky soil and arid climate. The Israelites had to learn the contours and local wisdom of the land to make the desert bloom. "They (the Israelites) managed to establish themselves in the steep, rocky hill country because it was the only part of the land of Canaan nobody else wanted. They survived as farmers by becoming intimate with their land, by learning to meet its expectations and its needs, and by passing on their knowledge, with each generation serving the human 'seed stock' indispensable for the well-being of the next generation."[2]

If you have not already watched the 2018 movie *The Biggest Little Farm,* stop what you are doing and find a way to view it. The movie tells the story of the transformation of Apricot Lane Farms in Moorpark, California, from a desolate, dried-up, dead farm to a flourishing oasis. The transformation took seven painful years. As the film progresses, you see the failures and successes of John and Molly Chester as they seek to make the farm viable. Sitting in the theater with my family, I kept thinking the transformation of this farm is just like the transformation of a local church: It takes a community, it takes determination, it takes vision, it takes luck, and it takes time, lots of time!

During every setback they experienced, I kept seeing in my head the two sentences of R. Robert Cueni I have posted on the wall of my office: "The experienced church leader has learned while renewing an established congregation may take only one half as many radical changes as projected, it will take twice as long as anticipated, and be three times more difficult than ever imagined. One can never overestimate the time and energy required."[3]

The approach of this book, a church on the move, is a slow-church approach; this is not an approach where one can flip a community of faith from fledging to flourishing overnight. This approach will take patience (the first characteristic of love in 1 Corinthians 13) and lots of time. Judson Church is slowly adapting, discovering, and embracing this approach. Slowly, I am learning that I do not have all the answers, and surprises are always around the corner. Slowly, I am beginning to know the sights and sounds and aromas and people of the community. By focusing on the goings-on inside the bikeable parish, I am discovering ways the beauty of Judson's witness can help the community, and I am discovering the beauty of the ways the community's witness can help Judson. We are seeking to be a part of the work of God already in our midst.

When I first started riding my bike to church, mine was the only one parked out front. After the church installed four bike racks, others started riding their bikes to worship on Sunday and preschool parents and children rode their bikes during the week. At first, I was the only one from my family who rode regularly. Now, seven years later, all five of us ride to work, to church, to school, to the grocery store. Walking, biking, and taking public transit grants my children a level of freedom I did not know growing up. My daughter, Seneca, walks, rides her bike, or takes the bus to school, to go thrifting with her friends, to work at the YMCA, and to social justice rallies at the state capitol in St. Paul. My oldest son, Glen, recently marched five miles from his high school to City Hall to protest gun violence. After the demonstration, the students were invited to take part in a discussion with city leaders. Glen had to make a decision: He could either skip the discussion and ride home with his friends or stay for the discussion without his friends and take the bus home. He stayed and took the bus home.

You need to know that Lori and I pay, or incentivize, our children to walk, ride bikes, and take public transit. When our kids turn sixteen, we give them an option: they can get their license and we will add them to our insurance, but allowance remains the same, $16 a month ($1 for every year), and they have to contribute to gas, insurance, and maintenance costs. Or they can wait until they are eighteen or older to get their license, and their allowance will rise to $16 + $50 + a monthly bus card + a new bike. That $50 a month is equivalent to the cost of adding a driver under eighteen to our insurance policy.

This arrangement was a no-brainer for Lori and me. I cannot stress enough the level of independence and freedom this arrangement has given our children. They are not dependent on their parents to shuttle them all over the Twin Cities. This also produces copious amounts of independence for Lori and me. We do not have to build our schedules around theirs. So far, each child has accepted the more money, monthly bus card, and new bike deal. Our insurance agent, however, is flummoxed!

The 2-3 Percent Rule of Social Change

Perhaps the most important element of church renewal and social justice is the 2-3 percent rule of social change. People want social change, especially, to happen immediately; I do too. I realize, however, that social change rarely, if ever, happens quickly. Christie Manning, assistant professor of Environmental Studies and Psychology at Macalester College in St. Paul, shared with me that if an individual, institution, or organization is seeking lasting social change, they need to plan to move the needle, or bend the arc, 2 to 3 percent each year. More than that and the social system cannot absorb the change and backlash occurs. Any less and the change is negligible and never noticed.

Seeking 2-3 percent social change each year may seem like an infinitesimal effort, but in ten years, 20 to 30 percent social change would be significant, groundbreaking, even otherworldly change. When churches slow down to the 2-3 percent pace of social change, they are present for the face-to-face, block-by-block, neighborhood-by-neighborhood needs and relationships. At this speed congregations can cultivate and nurture the relationships that enable lasting social change. Walking, biking, and taking public transit may not be the fastest way to get from point A to point B, but they are more relationship-efficient and provide more serendipitous moments and more opportunities to engage in the 2-3 percent realm of social change.

My personal goal for Judson Church is to have 10 percent of the congregation walking, biking, or taking public transit on Sundays (and in their daily lives) within five years. From the margins, this small mass of people can radically change how a congregation lives out its mission. Ten percent can provide critical mass. Ten percent changes the experience from *I'm the only one walking, biking or taking public transit* to *I'm part of a movement* (pun intended).[4] This transformation will not follow a clear and crisp plan of 2 percent growth each year, culminating in an even 10 percent growth in the fifth year. Instead, there may not be any growth, the first two years and rapid growth in years three, four, and five. The goal is for the transformation to happen gradually as the church encourages others to be a part of this movement.

All that has to happen for social change to start is for someone to initiate change. It doesn't take much. Ecuadorian farmer Omar Tello says that to regenerate one hundred hectares of rainforest, you only need to plant three or four hectares because the seeds will spread and the fecundity of the land will suffice;[5] or maybe you start with 1 percent. Gandhi and other Hindu practitioners believed if only 1 percent of the world's population practiced meditation, there would be world peace.

You can probably even go smaller than 1 percent. In 2016 artists Anders Swanson and Torrin Swanson had the idea of importing one hundred Dutch plain bikes in a shipping container from the Netherlands to Winnipeg, Manitoba, Canada. Their scheme was to drop a "culture bomb" of Dutch bikes into the city to transform the way people in Winnipeg experienced both bicycling and their bicycles. Plain bikes, or *omafiets* (literally "grandmother bikes"), are upright, boring, step-through, heavy, steel bikes outfitted with lights, fenders, a chain guard, a front basket, rear racks, and a bell. They are not bikes for racing or even serious exercise; they are transit bikes, or as the Dutch would say, a form of faster walking. Pedalers do not wear special outfits but regular clothes, work clothes (suits and dresses). In four years organizers have imported three shipments of bicycles, delivering 680+ Dutch bikes to the citizens of Winnipeg (a city of 750,000) or roughly .01 percent of the population. Already they have changed the city, bike culture, and the experience of bicycle transit.[6]

Please note that although the Dutch do have a rich history of bicycling, it was their response to the 1970s oil crisis that generated their modern bicycle culture. One of the ways bicycling culture took root was the national policy of "Car-Free Sundays." What if churches tried to initiate Car-Free Sundays as part of our mission? Sunday mornings are great days to ride bikes to church because of the decrease in traffic. Another possibility would be a car-free worship weekend. I have tried, unsuccessfully, to include "bike to worship" as part of Bike Week in Minneapolis. My goal is to have Islamic, Jewish, and Christian and other faith worshippers' bike to their services. One weekend of interfaith bicycling (or walking or taking public transit) would change the worship experience for everyone and the neighborhood and the city!

Take my friends Jeff and Sino in Southern California, who a few years ago enrolled their queer family (two dads and one daughter) at a local karate studio a few years ago. Instantly the karate studio changed from a homogenous white heterosexual studio to a diverse studio. Even if just one family or one person chooses to walk, bike, or take public transit to church, that act will change the congregation. If one committee initiates an intentional relationship with a BIPOC organization, if one member leans into a relationship with someone who does not look or love or believe like they do, change, slow and meaningful change will come.

Yeah, But . . .

Even as you adopt a slow church posture and implement the 2-3 percent rule of social change, there is still not enough time. If you think you can do this all by yourself, you cannot. The church on the move project, however, is not a solo project; it is not a pastor-centered or council-centered project, it is a both/and/ and then some project. It is a creative cooperation between the pastor and church leaders, church community and the neighborhood/community/parish. Next, I will share alternative ways to structure time and energy to be a church on the move.

Church Leaders and Core Volunteers as "Staff"

One day I was praying, "God, I need help, I cannot turn around Judson Church all by myself." There was no answer. Later that day as I was rehearsing my sermon, facing an empty sanctuary, I began to envision the people who would be present on Sunday morning. Then the answer came to me in the form of a question: "What if some of the people in the pews were the 'staff' you had been looking for?"

A few days later Rich called and wanted to get together. Over coffee, Rich, a retired banker, revealed to me that he had always wanted to be a minister, but because he is gay, the doors to ministry were always shut. He told me, "My goal in retirement is to help as many churches as possible to become more LGBTQIA+ as possible. When you don't see me on Sunday mornings, it is not because I'm sleeping in, but because I'm at other churches teaching, preaching, and bearing witness." I replied that this sounded like a ministry! At the next church council meeting, I presented the idea of making Rich our Welcoming and Affirming Minister. They voted yes, and the next Sunday the congregation voted yes too! A few weeks later, we ordained and charged Rich with three missions: one, to help Judson continue and deepen its LGBTQIA+ work. In this capacity Rich initiates and nurtures relationships with LGBTQIA+ organizations such as The Aliveness Project, Our Front Minnesota, Clare Housing, and Twin Cities Pride; two, to respond to individuals and families seeking help and consolation concerning LGBTQIA+ matters or concerns; three, to help, encourage, and counsel other churches in the Twin Cities and beyond to become Welcoming and Affirming.[7] Do we pay Rich? No, but we do provide him with business cards and an email address.

Or take Polly. She is the chair of the Worship Committee at Judson Church. She is an artistic retired woman who, I believe, would have pursued a call to ministry if she had been given the opportunity earlier in life. During a worship committee meeting, I made this plea: "Folks, I'm running out of ideas and energy. If anyone could help develop the call to worship, I would be much obliged." The next morning Polly emailed me one of the greatest calls to worship I had ever read. I asked if she had another; she did, and another! This relationship has blossomed into beautiful expressions each Sunday of art and rituals with a wider inclusion of the congregation.

Just like moving into the neighborhood began to transform Judson Church, so too did moving into the congregation transform our staff. Rich and Polly both attend our weekly staff meetings, and both share insights into aspects of Judson's ministry. Their energy and love and passion enable Judson to function as bigger than it really is. If we operated solely from the perspective of staff being only full-time ordained clergy, then our model couldn't survive.

Their energy has also encouraged other members of the community to take on more staff-like functions. While Brad was the moderator, he recognized a need for communication and marketing. When his one-year term as moderator ended, he did not run as far as possible from church work. He started a Communications Taskforce, asked the church council for $1,000 to hire a college communications major as an intern to help coordinate our efforts, and invited others to help in this endeavor. Brad's successor, Laura, saw a need for a solstice celebration of community, candle-lighting, songs, and poetry. She did not wait for the staff to create the program; she asked us to help her form it.

Sunday School Teachers

Every summer the Christian Education committee meets and prays that someone in the congregation will hear the Spirit of God inviting them to become a Sunday School teacher. And every year the Spirit of God doesn't seem to move anyone. But as I read *Real Good Church: How Our Church Came Back from the Dead and Yours Can, Too* by Molly Phinney Baskette, I started to see that maybe we were going about our prayers in the wrong way. Instead of waiting for the Spirit to invite someone to teach, what if we advertised, hired, and paid someone to teach?[8] Everyone wants the Sunday School program to thrive, everyone wants their kids, grandkids, and neighborhood kids to be in the Sunday School program, but no one can commit to thirty-five to forty Sundays a year, and in many small city-neighborhood churches there simply are not the people to make this happen. Paying Sunday School teachers sounded, at first, like heresy, but the more the parents and members of the Christian Education committee thought about it, the more it morphed from heresy to genius! We did not have funds in the budget to hire a full-time (or even part-time) Christian education staff person, but we did have funds to pay for a Sunday School teacher, in particular for Our Whole Lives (OWL, a series of sexuality education programs for all age groups).[9]

Taking Rev. Baskette's lead, Judson Church started looking outside the church membership for teachers. Instantly, the search went from "the Spirit isn't moving anyone to teach" to "How do we decide who to hire from the list of applicants?" We found our OWL teacher quite easily; she was already a friend/neighbor of the congregation, a trained leader, and a professional sexual education teacher. Hiring an outside member to be the OWL teacher did more than providing our youth with an amazing program; it also freed the congregation from applying the notion of "exclusive rights" for paid staff. The OWL teacher first worships at a nearby Lutheran Church with her family, then walks to Judson to teach. The staffing model memory of the congregation was full-time staff who worked exclusively for Judson and were integral to the everyday life of the community. Even though most of the staff does not work solely at Judson, the staff model memory still permeated. The choir director at Judson teaches at the University of Minnesota and directs the Norwegian worship service at Mindekirken following Judson's worship; the children's and youth coordinator at Judson is also a spiritual director at the Loyola Spirituality Center; the Judson facilities manager owns a housing repair business and works for the church on a contract basis, coming in when needed.

This approach to church staffing has been a win-win for the congregation. On the one hand, it has freed more time for me to be involved in community ministry. On the other hand, it has enabled core volunteers to contribute their gifts and talents to the life of the congregation.

Furthermore, by hiring Sunday School teachers, for the first time in years, members of the Christian Education committee can attend coffee hour, participate in Adult Education opportunities or simply socialize in the back of the sanctuary after worship, all of which were not possible under our previous model.

Accidental Exercise: Embracing Two-fers

Walking, biking, and taking public transit made me rethink how I used my hours. I used to look at Google Maps for the time it took to walk, or bike, or take public transit from point A to point B, and say there is simply not enough time, it's quicker to drive. In a single day I could not do visits, administrative work, study, and exercise! But what if you could do two at the same time?

If you are walking or pedaling to work, school, or church or doing errands in the bikeable parish, you can easily get from point A to point B on a bike and get in thirty minutes of "accidental exercise." Rather than sitting passively behind the wheel of a car, you can actively walk or pedal to your destination. The World Health Organization recommends that the average adult perform moderate exercise for 150 minutes a week, or thirty minutes five days a week. One time my pastoral colleague, the Rev. Doug Donley at University Baptist Church in Minneapolis, and I rode our bikes to a local pub. When we got there I asked him how often he rode. He replied, "Every chance I get." Then he pointed to his slim midsection and said with a smile, "Riding this bike is my form of *girth control*."

In his book *Street Smart*, Sam Schwartz, an American traffic engineer, quotes from the 1928 book *Walking* by George Macauley Trevelyan: "I have two doctors: My left leg and my right. When my body and mind are out of gear . . . I know that I shall have only to call in my two doctors to be well again."[10] One of the best investments I have made was a $40 indestructible, weatherproof, Bluetooth speaker that attaches to my bike handlebars. While I ride, I can listen to podcasts and lectures or make phone calls. You can do this in a car too, but there is no beneficial exercise taking place. You can listen or make phone calls on a treadmill, but that is not transit. Only while riding a bike or walking can you exercise and transit and study—and reduce your carbon footprint, with no need to pay for gasoline or a gym membership!

Another way to incorporate exercise into your work life is to invite others to walk with you around the neighborhood. There is something about movement and fresh air and the rhythm of the body that opens up new possibilities. Whenever I am stuck and cannot solve the crossword puzzle, I go take a walk. Whenever the kids and I are at loggerheads, I ask them to go on a walk with me. Whenever a parishioner is hurt or frustrated or down, I ask them to join me on a walk. Whenever someone comes to the church seeking spiritual direction, I ask if they will walk with me.

Micro Sabbaticals

I used to look at a map and view the distance and time from Judson to nursing homes in the outlying cities as insurmountable. There was no way I could visit and still read all the articles or chapters of books needed for sermon preparation. Then I started bringing magazine and journal articles and books with me on the bus as I rode out to the nursing homes. The time spent on the bus was quieter, with fewer interruptions and disturbances than two hours in my study at church. Please do not think all buses and trains are fortresses of silence; they are not. But gradually I learned to budget my time more effectively and to plan accordingly.

For the past few years, Amtrak has offered a writing residency on its long-distance routes. Up to fifteen writers have been awarded tickets and on board lodging for a week. The program gifts the writers space and time to reflect and write, but also "a travel experience with amazing scenery, an environment that fosters engaging connections, and the ability to explore and be inspired by the diversity of landscapes America has to offer."[11]

Before moving on to sermon writing, I want to offer a cautionary word of advice: not everything goes according to plan. You will be late you will arrive sweaty you will end up in the wrong place. But over time you and the congregation will adjust. More on being late in the next chapter.

Sermon Writing

One day while perusing the stacks at the library of United Seminary of the Twin Cities, I noticed a book from 1973 with a catchy, gimmicky title: *How to Find Time for Better Preaching and Better Pastoring* by Joseph McCabe. Arrogantly, I picked it up, thinking I would scoff at the contents but quickly became mesmerized by the author's proposal, a method to free up ten Sundays of preaching preparation time in order to devote 100 hours to pastoring. His method centered on three ideas: One, every six to eight weeks the preacher lists in the bulletin the sermon titles from the previous six to eight weeks so the congregation can vote on their favorite, and then the preacher repeats that sermon (this happens four times a year). His premise is sound: We watch movies more than once, listen to the same song multiple times, and are we really sure the listeners listened the first time? Two, the pastor and another pastor in the community exchange pulpits four times a year. This gives both congregations an opportunity to hear another voice and develop deeper relationships within the community. If the other pastor is not a strong preacher, you will be more grateful for your preacher. If the other pastor is a strong preacher, then your pastor may have to devote more time to the craft. Three, the preacher preaches two sermons a year by a figure in Christian history (Julian of Norwich or Gardner Taylor).

If we are going to develop new and deeper relationships within the community, we have to think creatively about how to best invest our time and energy in the service of the church and community. This model offers one way to look at time from a different angle to promote good preaching and good pastoring. In the 100 hours created by this program, the pastor can freely look for avenues to volunteer and establish new relationships. We know nature abhors a vacuum, and unless you are diligent about guarding these one hundred hours over ten weeks, others will find ways to fill them up.

A few years ago, Carol Howard Merritt asked in *The Christian Century*, "What if we saw the church in service to the world, and our work outside of the church as a necessity? What if every pastor spent one day a week in service to the larger community? It could change our ministries, and our churches."[12] I love her idea, but I cannot spare an entire day. I do, however, block off two afternoons a week for intentional neighborhood/community/parish work. I have communicated with the church council and congregation about my community work as movement work. Each council meeting, I give a report about my conversations and findings.

Another possibility is to invite members of the church and members of the community to preach once a quarter.

110 Conversations: The Door-to-Door Alternative

Okay, you have started walking, biking, and taking public transit. You have started to read, study, and pray while doing these activities. You have learned to take phone calls on your bike and downloaded podcasts, sermons, and lectures to listen to. You have started to rethink how you can reuse a sermon, or partner with another church to share worship planning. You have embraced the slow church movement. You have welcomed members of the church and community as core volunteers and staff. Right at this moment someone will come forward and recommend that the church engage in a door-to-door visitation program. Author Tony Campolo does just that in his book *Revolution and Renewal: How Churches Are Saving Our Cities.* "Visiting door-to-door is where we have to begin. If we are going to turn things around in urban America, we have to make contact with the people in the neighborhoods that surround our churches."[13]

As much as I love Tony Campolo, I disagree with a door-to-door evangelism program. I have tried this approach and found it wanting. I have found neighbors and families who are exhausted by front-door solicitors. I have found neighbors and families distrustful of anyone from a religious institution. But all is not lost; there are alternatives to a door-to-door visitation program, including alley walks, prayer walks around the neighborhood, card tables set up out front with a "The Pastor Is In" sign, and coffee shop office hours. The most effective alternative to the door-to-door visitation program I have found is intentional, one-to-one conversations. Rather than meet people when it is most convenient for the church (a door-to-door visitation program), meet neighbors when it is most convenient for them (intentional one-to-one scheduled conversations).

In 2018 I heard the Rev. David Van Brakle, who at the time served as pastor of Wilmette Community Church outside of Chicago, describe how he conducted one hundred one-on-one interviews with people from the community. As Judson Church's 110th birthday approached, I thought I would like to conduct 110 conversations. I contacted David to see how he did it. His only advice was this: Start with one community/neighborhood leader, and when you end the conversation, ask the person for two or three recommendations for who you should talk with next. With this information in mind, I set out to mark Judson's 110th year of existence by conducting 110 one-on-one interviews with community members—specifically, those who were not from Judson Church. I gave myself a year to complete this endeavor; unfortunately, the pandemic prevented me from doing the full 110. Normally I would have been upset about not reaching my goal, but the results from the conversations outweighed any feelings of disappointment.

After three or four initial interviews, I centered on these four questions. **One**, do you know where Judson Church is located? Because most people from the neighborhood had no idea where Judson Church is located. **Two**, do you know anything about Judson Church? Because if they knew anything about the church, it was either that we were the church with the playground or we were the church with the preschool. **Three**, what are your biggest worries about life and living in this neighborhood? (When my oldest son was entering kindergarten, the teacher asked him, "What do you like to do?" and my kid just looked at her. But when she asked, "What are you afraid of?" he responded, "Bears, bats, monsters." Ever since, I ask people about their worries before their hopes). **Four**, if you had a chance to tell the church where they should direct their energies, what would you wish they would focus on? (I still cannot believe how earnest and sincere the respondents were to this question). I finished each interview by asking for permission to take their picture and asking whom they would recommend I talk to next. I conducted all the interviews in the same coffee shop.

What I learned was sobering and insightful. I learned that neighbors who live on the same block as the church had no idea where it was or anything about it! They knew where Judson Preschool was, but they had no idea a church was associated with it. One neighbor who lives within a nine-iron shot of Judson talked about how much they liked the yellow Adirondack chairs in our front yard. Two problems with that: One, we don't have any yellow Adirondack chairs, and two, we don't have a front yard. This neighbor mistook Judson Church for St. Luke's Episcopal Church.

In normal circumstances, mistaking a Baptist church for an Episcopal church would be the highest compliment.[14] In this circumstance, however, it was not a compliment; it was a serious problem. The neighbor's mistake proved to me that Judson Church had identity problems. Not only was our building not communicating our values, our building wasn't communicating at all!

I once heard someone quote Paul Tillich, who said, "The culture asks the questions and the church provides the answers." My research at the coffee shop proved that the church was answering questions no one was asking. I also discovered a generation of neighbors who couldn't tell the difference between Baptists and Lutherans; not surprising, but they didn't know the difference between Lutherans and Catholics either. In their minds, they were all part of one big institution. One neighbor did not know Christians could be pro-LGBTQIA+; another neighbor loved the rainbow flags hanging from our building, but thought we were naive Christians who did not know the symbolism of the flag and instead just liked the colors.

The conversations showed me that if Judson Church continues to venture into the neighborhood, the possibilities for growth (name recognition, trust, ministries) were endless. Because the data collected emerged from a conversation, Judson Church had the ability to go deeper than the usual ministry plan. For example, when I asked the neighbors about their worries, they freely listed their worries and fears: gentrification, rising home prices, racial disparities, youth mental health, environmental issues. All would be at the top of the list in any neighborhood in America, but when I asked if they could flesh out these fears and worries, I received pain-filled responses: "I don't know my neighbors," "I'm alone," "I want my kids to be able to walk to school safely," "I feel helpless to do anything about the environment or racial justice," "I'm exhausted."

Every month I would compile a list of who I talked with, what I learned and who I hoped to talk to next and reported it to Judson Church council. At first, they didn't believe our neighbors didn't know anything about the church. They couldn't believe someone thought we didn't know what the rainbow flags meant. And they refused to believe our neighbors knew more about the playground than what went on in the church building. But each month I kept sharing these stories in emails, newsletters, sermons, and council minutes. The meeting before the pandemic ceased in-person worship, three members of the council offered, "I think I'm going to start doing this too!"

For years I sat in my office and dreamed about what I thought the community wanted or needed. Never did I think I could just ask them. For years, the church councils where I served, and I cooked up programs and messages we thought would attract the neighbors. Never did we think to just ask them. The conversations were an exercise in slow church. They took many hours over the course of months. Each conversation took at least an hour to conduct, plus the time it took to set them up via email, texting, and phone calls. But they were worth every second. Our ministry at Judson Church is now more focused and is directed not by what we think others need and want, but by what they have told us they need and want. Or to put it another way, maybe we are starting to smell like the neighborhood! In a homily to priests on Maundy Thursday 2013, Pope Francis asked the priests to "be shepherds, with the 'odor of the sheep,' make it real, as shepherds among your flock."[15] Taking on the odor of the sheep takes time and proximity, and vulnerability (someone has put their own skin and heart on the line).

When churches ceased in-person worship services in the Twin Cities due to the COVID-19 pandemic, Judson Church was well-positioned to respond because of our conversations, our discernment, and our relationships. We knew our neighbors and we knew our community needs. We focused on connections, communications, and responding to emergency needs. When the uprisings took place after the killing of George Floyd, Judson Church was ready to respond because of our conversations, our discernment, and our relationships. When we put out a call for donations to help those in need of housing, food, and medical attention, we collected and disbursed over $40,000 in two weeks. We knew exactly where to give the funds because of the previous months of listening and responding. In a pattern revealed before in this book, the neighborhood also reached out to the church. Neighbors called to tell me the night the church was spray-painted and when someone tried to start a fire on our front steps, and suggested we leave the lights on during the night. When I was walking the sidewalks in the immediate area of the church, they told me they too were keeping an eye on the building.

The Coffee Shop as an Auxiliary Office/Study/Studio

"110 Conversations" did the one thing I needed to do but couldn't name: It forced me out of the office and provided me the space and time to listen to the community. As stated earlier, I do not think it is the best investment of resources to have the pastor, church staff, and leaders always inside the church building. There are tasks that have to be done at the church office, but most tasks can be done elsewhere.

Have you ever tabulated how much time you or your pastor spend in the office? For two weeks, keep track of how much time you spend in your office. The church office is a great place to read, study, think, write, dream, counsel, pray, make phone calls, design Sunday services, etc. For the record, I love my church offices—plural is correct. I have a public office near the other staff offices and copy machine and mail slots and coffee pot, and a private office upstairs with a fireplace, bookshelves, my record player, and my favorite chair. Given the choice, I would gladly stay upstairs with a cup of hot chocolate, a jazz record playing, writing a sermon. But the office prevents me from being out of the church building and among people in the neighborhood/community/parish.

While attending a workshop offered by John Pentland, pastor of Hillhurst United Church of Canada in Calgary, Alberta, on his book *Fishing Tips: How Curiosity Transformed a Community of Faith*, a colleague of his stood up and said, "You've never seen a pastor's office as clean as John's. It's not that he is a neat freak. It's because he is never in it! He is always out in the community and mostly working at the neighborhood coffee shop."[16] Pentland's friend reminded me of Pope Francis' instruction to the Rev. Konrad Krajewski, the Vatican almoner, the person in charge of distributing alms on behalf of the pope: "You can sell your desk. You don't need it. You need to get out of the Vatican. Don't wait for people to come ringing. You need to go out and look for the poor."[17]

Pentland went on to describe coffee shops as the neighborhood's living room. As he spoke, I thought of all the times people have opened up about their lives; the conversations took place in living rooms, not church offices. Pastoral colleagues Jonathan Malone, Mindi Melton-Mitchell, and Stacey Simpson-Duke haven't sold their desks, but they have started a new discipline of having open office hours at local coffee shops. The time and location of their hours are announced in the church bulletin and shared on social media. They make themselves available to both the church community and the neighborhood. The church community recognizes them as their pastors, but the neighborhood mostly does not know who they are until they place a "Pastor Is In" or "Free Prayer" sign on their laptops or tables. This arrangement has led to people asking for prayer, asking questions about the Bible, and asking about the pastors' sermons. It is one clever way to get yourself out of the church office while at the same time getting "church/office" work done. They have also found church members more readily available to meet at the coffee shop than at the church. I inherited the church model of "Build it and they will come." But my (almost) 110 conversations revealed to me: "They have no idea you are there." My colleagues are showing a way of entering into the neighborhood's living room and having spiritual conversations. We cannot wait for people to find the church; the church needs to find them.

Another way of getting out of the office and finding people is offered by the Rev. Gregory Fryer, co-pastor of Immanuel Lutheran Church in New York City. He took inspiration from

Peanuts comic strip and opened his own "outdoor pastoral counseling center." With a desk, chair, and signs reading "Spiritual Help 5¢" and "The Pastor Is In," he set up shop on the corner of East 88th and Lexington Avenue. In an interview with *The Christian Post*, he said, "Not only do I hope that more churches will do this, but also that each of us, as individuals, will do it, too. This is a form of love we can provide for our neighbors: that we will make ourselves available to listen as carefully as we can and then to answer in a godly and encouraging way."[18]

All of the materials covered in this chapter take time. Moving out into the community takes time. Setting up an "auxiliary office" at the coffee shop takes time. Having 110 one-on-one conversations takes time. Living by the 2-3 percent rule takes time. Being part of a movement for change takes time. However, I have found that once trust is established within the congregation and neighborhood and with the congregants and neighbors, change will move fast, but it takes time to arrive at that point.

Prayer, in the Spirit of Mother Teresa

People will say walking, bicycling, and taking public transit are
unreasonable, irrational, and slow. Do them anyway.
If you are kind with your staff, building, and money, people
may accuse you of selfish, ulterior motives. Be kind anyway.
If you are successful meeting and befriending your neighbors,
you will win some unfaithful friends and some genuine
enemies. Succeed anyway.
If you are honest and sincere with people you meet on foot and
while pedaling and taking public transit, some may deceive
you. Be honest and sincere anyway.
When you arrive at a gathering refreshed and connected and
happy because you walked, cycled or took public transit,
some may be jealous. Be happy anyway.
All the reductions of your carbon footprint will often be
forgotten. Reduce it anyway. Give the best you have, and it
will never be enough. Give your best anyway.
In the final analysis, it is between you and God. Amen.

Experiment: Meals on Wheels Delivery

Every week volunteers from around the metro area arrive at Judson Church to pick up meals for delivery as part of the Meals on Wheels program. About 99 percent of the volunteers drive cars for this noble project, but one deliverer, Zan Ceeley, delivers meals on her bicycle. Attached to her bike is a trailer she used to haul her kids in, but now she uses to haul meals. One day I biked alongside Zan as food was delivered.

In one hour we delivered meals to six customers in South Minneapolis. Delivering the meals by bike was faster than by car because of parking and traffic, but it was not a speedy experience.

Zan revealed parts of my neighborhood I had walked, biked, and driven past many times but never noticed. From the outside the homes looked normal and happy, but once the doors opened you could feel the loneliness and isolation seep out. For many people on her list, Zan is the only person they see or come in contact with during the week. In one hour, I had a host guide me through the neighborhood and introduce me to neighbors. In one hour, my understanding of Judson's neighbors and the neighborhood was altered. There is time.

Questions for Reflection

1. How many hours a week do you spend in the church office?

2. How many hours a week do you invest outside of the church office?

3. What organizations could you partner with for an hour, for a day, to get to know your neighbors and neighborhood more? Meals on Wheels? Police ride-along? Community board member of local YMCA?

4. What coffee shop could you start occupying as your auxiliary office?

5. Pick one of the Gospels and mark down how much time Jesus spent "in the office." Indeed, Jesus invented time, praying, fixing meals, dealing with interruptions, etc. But how much time is he on the road? On his way to somewhere? At a crossroads?

6. How many steps do you take each day? How many of those steps are in and around your church's neighborhood? Who could you ask from your neighborhood to walk with you on your daily journeys?

7. On a nice day, grab a chair from the Fellowship Hall and take it outside of your church. Sit in that chair along the sidewalk for an hour and see what happens. Who walks by? Seniors getting exercise? Kids getting out of the house? Middle-aged people listening to podcasts? How many people walk by? Who interacts? Who ignores? Who is walking a dog? What are the dogs' names?

8. What is your practice/observance of the Sabbath? What do you wish it looked like?

9. Who would be the first person you would contact for your one hundred one-to-one conversations?

10. What would be your four questions?

Recipe: Cold Fried Chicken

One day a friend told me about the practice of the Scandinavian power lunch: Executives and colleagues have lunch together in the meeting, but they all bring their own lunches from home—they brown-bag it! Here is a simple suggestion for a Scandinavian power lunch. The next time you are at a grocery store that has a prepared foods section, buy some freshly fried chicken but do not eat it right away. Instead, once home, place the fried chicken in the refrigerator and do not touch it till the next morning. One of the greatest missed opportunities in life is the experience of eating cold fried chicken for lunch (or for a snack or for dinner).

Vegetarian Option: Beet Salad

Take two beets, or three depending on their size, wash, and trim the ends. Place one cup of water in electric pressure cooker, set tray in the water, and place the beets on the tray. Close the lid and the vent. Cook on high pressure for 25 or 30 minutes (the beauty of a beet is that you cannot overcook it).

Once done, remove from pot and cool. Peel and cut into sizes you appreciate. Toss with lettuce, toasted walnuts, and blue cheese dressing, and voila, a power lunch for the ages.

But here is another alternative: beet sliders. Slice the beets into hamburger-sized slices rather than diced. Warm butter in an iron skillet and fry the beet slices for 2–3 minutes per side. Serve on a pretzel bun with blue cheese dressing and voila, another fantastic power lunch!

Suggested Reading List

Allan, Nicolas. *Jesus' Day Off* (London: Red Fox, 2001). A children's book recommended by Kirk Byron Jones!

Baskette, Molly Phinney. *Real Good Church: How Our Church Came Back from the Dead, and Yours Can, Too* (Cleveland, OH: Pilgrim, 2014).

Bruntlett, Melissa and Chris. *Building the Cycling City: The Dutch Blueprint for Urban Living* (Washington: Island Press, 2018).

Ekelund, Torbjørn. *In Praise of Paths: Walking Through Time and Nature* (Vancouver: Greystone, 2020).

Jones, Kirk Byron. *Rest in the Storm: Self-Care Strategies for Clergy and Other Caregivers, 20th Anniversary Edition* (Valley Forge, PA: Judson, 2021). Honestly, any and every book by Kirk Byron Jones is worth your time and reading edification.

McCabe, Joseph E. *How to Find Time for Better Preaching and Better Pastoring* (Philadelphia, PA: Westminster, 1973).

Pattison, John and Smith, Chris. *Slow Church: Cultivating Community in the Patient Way of Jesus* (Downers Grove, IL: IVP, 2014).

The Biggest Little Farm documentary film centered on the turnaround of a farm in California using permaculture practices. © 2018. Can be viewed on many online platforms.

NOTES

1. CAUTION: I often hear people complain that churches move at a glacial pace. When I preached a sermon series based on the book *Slow Church: Cultivating Community in the Patient Way of Jesus* (IVP Books, 2014), some congregants scoffed, "aren't we slow enough already?" Be prepared for pushback when you propose this idea.

2. Ellen Davis, *Scripture, Culture and Agriculture: An Agrarian Reading of the Bible* (New York: Cambridge, 2009), 38.

3. R. Robert Cueni, *Dinosaur Heart Transplants: Renewing Mainline Congregations* (Nashville, TN: Abingdon, 2000), 55.

4. Samuel I. Schwartz, *Street Smart* (New York: Public Affairs, 2015), 13. His research shows that "the Millennials haven't stopped driving. They've just slowed down. No reasonable prediction suggests anything but a change at the margin: instead of 85 to 90 percent of all travel by automobile, perhaps 'only' 75 percent or so. But that 10 percent difference is hugely significant. It will determine how much of our national income should be invested in highways, and how much in subways, how much in sprawl, and how much in density. Entirely because of this marginal change, the future looks a lot more like the pre-automobile past. Only better. Easier to navigate, more accessible, and definitely safer, for pedestrians, transit users, and drivers. You know: smarter. The consequences are gigantic, especially for those cities and towns that want to be part of that future."

5. Jo Mathys, "Regrowing the Rainforest" March 31, 2020, People Fixing the World, BBC Podcast, https://www.bbc.co.uk/programmes/p08853y8.

6. Erin Riediger, *Plain Bicycle*, six episodes. April 26, 2020–May 31, 2020. Listen for the full and wonderful story of this scheme, https://www.plainbicycle.org.

7. American Baptist polity allows for "local ordinations." This ordination is only recognized within the context of the locally ordaining church body and does not have national recognition.

8. Molly Phinney Baskette, *Real Good Church: How Our Church Came Back from the Dead and Yours Can, Too* (Cleveland, OH: Pilgrim, 2014), 29.

9. See https://www.ucc.org/justice_sexuality-education_our-whole-lives.

10. Schwartz, *Street Smart*, 94.

11. See https://media.amtrak.com/2016/07/amtrak-residency-program-selects-writers/.

12. Carol Howard Merritt, "Reaching Out or Caving In?" *The Christian Century*, November 19, 2014, https://www.christiancentury.org/blogs/archive/2014-11/reaching-out-or-caving.

13. Tony Campolo, *Revolution and Renewal: How Churches Are Saving Our Cities* (Louisville, KY: Westminster John Knox, 2004), 64.

14. I frequently use a moniker from the late Rev. Peter Gomes, minister at Harvard's Memorial Church, who described himself as a Baptist with an Anglican Oversoul.

15. Pope Francis, Homily of Pope Francis, preached March 28, 2013, http://www.vatican.va/content/francesco/en/homilies/2013/documents/papa-francesco_20130328 _messa-crismale.html.

16. "Fishing Tips Workshop" September 18, 2018, in the Fellowship Hall of Baptist Temple, Rochester, NY.

17. Nicole Winfield, "Pope ramps up charity office to be near poor, sick," November 28, 2013, https://apnews.com/article/cb4d2cbd-01084073b16acec30232bad0.

18. Brandon Showalter, "Lutheran Pastor Inspired by 'Peanuts' Takes Spiritual Council to Streets of New York." December 2, 2016, https://www.christianpost.com/news/lutheran-pastor-inspired-by-peanuts-takes-spiritual-counsel- to-streets-of-new-york-171855/.

Chapter 5
Embracing Risk

This book has provided a way for you and your congregation to move into your neighborhood/community/parish. Next will come the difficult part: actually doing it. There will be many obstacles and institutional forces trying to prevent you from trying these ideas. Know upfront that you will make mistakes, you will say the wrong thing on numerous occasions, and the only appropriate response will be a facepalm. Nevertheless, this is not the time to play it safe; this is a time to embrace risk. I would suggest you intentionally plan to take risks and to make mistakes! Church consultant and pastor Rev. Michael Piazza even recommends "churches should write into the pastor's contract the requirement to have twelve failures a year."[1]

I know your lips are probably going numb and your hands are ice-cold after reading that last paragraph, but look at our recent experiences during the pandemic. One of the blessings of online worship for churches during COVID-19 was the constant sea of mistakes and failures. It did not matter if the church was small or large, rich or poor, solo-pastored or multi-staffed; we all took risks and made mistakes and failed as we tried to adapt to online worship. I watched a pastor's robe catch fire (he was not injured), I watched a pastor preach while her kids danced and rolled and wrestled behind her; I watched a priest preach a homily unaware that his iPhone filters were making him look like Chewbacca, then Yoda, then Darth Vader. These common experiences finally allowed the freedom to laugh at ourselves, which in turn created the freedom to experiment, risk, and create.

We should have been taking more risks all along. We should have been encouraged by our scriptures to take risks. Think of Sarah laughing at God or Jacob wrestling the angel, or the prophet Jeremiah walking around with an iron yoke on his neck or the prophet Isaiah walking naked and barefoot or Jesus' risky invitation: "Follow me and I will make you fishers of people."

This is a book full of risks and risk-takers, but we do not view the Bible as an impetus for risk-taking; we view it as a book of endorsing the status quo. It took reading an op-ed in the *New York Times* by comedian Emily Winter, "I Got Rejected 101 Times,"[2] before I started embracing and preaching on risk.

In barely a thousand words, Winter described a year of seeking out one hundred rejections. After reading the essay I realized how much fear was holding me back from my work as a pastor and how much fear was holding the congregation back from their work as a church. The genius of her adventure to embrace risk was not that her career suddenly blossomed and took off (it didn't), but how embracing risk moved her career forward. Taking risks allowed her to land gigs that would have been perceived as out of reach if she had been ensnared by the fear of rejection.

Many times, I have been in church meetings and heard wonderful, beautiful and amazing ideas offered by members and seen those wonderful, beautiful, and amazing ideas snuffed out in a matter of seconds. Every time this happens, I see the interest and enthusiasm for the church shrink and atrophy. The most saddening part is not that the other members didn't like the idea or weren't inspired by the idea or didn't feel it was from God; instead, they would rather extinguish a creative idea than take a risk. As you move out into the community, you will take risks, you will risk rejection, and you will risk failure. Over time you will find that the more risks you are willing to take, the easier it will be to take more and bolder risks. Risk begets risk. What follows is not a risk management manual but risk encouragement prompts.

Risk Starting Small

Judson Church had a history of creating amazing ministry ideas with lots of startup energy and no plans for following through. Time after time they would watch great ideas fizzle to nothing. This repeated experience caused the congregation to be risk-averse. Time and again I would hear, "We tried that, but nothing happened." That refrain is the tell-tale sign of a church with no self-confidence.

Several years ago I was part of the First Parish Project, a Lilly-funded program aimed at pastors under thirty-five. The program sought to provide young pastors with the tools and experiences and relationships to succeed throughout their careers in the pastorate. Midway through the two-year program, we were introduced to the concept of church visioning. The leaders of the program found that most churches have a terrible track record of success: They start too big, they wander from their goals, they set timetables too far into the future. Their angle on church visioning was unique and specific: Start small, stay focused, and never plan for anything that will take a year or longer to finish. The logic behind their practice was simple: Success begets success.

For example, rather than saying we want to get to net-zero carbon by 2050, on the Sunday before Earth Day, invite people to walk, ride their bicycles, or take public transit to church. Expect people to resist this practical, simple, and manageable proposal. They will say it is not bold enough or that the act is meaningless; carry on. This invitation will need to be issued several weeks in advance to secure success. Why? Some people will need to tune their bikes (put air in the tires and oil the chains), some people will need to find their bikes, some people will need to figure out and test the best bike route from home to church. Some people will need to figure out how to get on the bus and what times the bus runs on a Sunday. Others will need to figure out the safest and best intersections to cross as they plan their walk. Encourage this kind of proactive planning.

When the Sunday comes and people do walk, pedal, or take public transit to church, cheer them on, give them a high-five, and celebrate the success in worship. Invite some to share their experiences. Risk begets risk and success begets success. Do not underestimate the power of one small success to spur more and larger acts within the congregation. Author Brian Doyle used to say that telling stories or sharing poems or novels, writing emails and texts, and giving talks or presentations could nudge the universe forward one millimeter.[3] When we tell stories and nudge one another forward one millimeter, when we create a culture of risk, we have the opportunity to move people to take action that they might not have on their own. Over time you will move to bigger and bolder acts. Over time you will begin to plan for events and programs two and three years in advance. Start small, take your time, accumulate small successes, and build your risk muscles.

Risk Cultural Status

By embracing risk, small city-neighborhood churches can let go of trying to attain cultural status. Let us start with a confessional: Small city-neighborhood churches are no longer (or never were) "notable churches or churches of note." Minneapolis/St. Paul is full of "notable churches or churches of note" like House of Hope Presbyterian, Westminster Presbyterian, Central Lutheran, Gloria Dei Lutheran, Hennepin Avenue United Methodist Church, or Plymouth Congregational. What do I mean by "churches of record?" The easiest way to explain it is for you to compare the front page of the *New York Times* and the front page of the *Wall Street Journal.* On the front page of the *New York Times,* you will find a page, above and below the fold, of "All the News That's Fit to Print." Look below the fold on the *Wall Street Journal* and you will find one quirky, out-of-place article with an italic headline. The headline may read, "UFO Spotting Has Replaced Bird Watching as Pandemic Obsession" or "Thirty-Year Game of Tag Continues" or "Resumes Are Starting to Look Like Instagram—and Sometimes Even Tinder." These are headlines of a column called "A-Hed," "where a story is light enough to float off the page where it resides."[4] The *Wall Street Journal* knows it is not the "paper of record," unlike the *Times;* therefore it can devote space to non-serious, bizarre, entertaining news on the front page.

Most, if not all, small city-neighborhood churches are not "churches of record" or churches of note or notable churches. Rather than lament this status, we should celebrate it. This lack of status is an invitation to embrace risk. Small city-neighborhood churches can operate under the cultural radar, moving out into the community and offering a faithful witness. What we lose by ceasing to acquire cultural status, we gain in authenticity.

An example of risking cultural status is none other than Pope Francis. In 2016 Franciscan Media published Italian journalist Rosario Carello's children's book, *Pope Francis Takes the Bus, and Other Unexpected Stories.* The book follows an acrostic pattern with stories for each letter of the alphabet. The genesis of the book emerged from all the stories of Archbishop Bergoglio, now Pope Francis, taking public transit in Argentina. This practice was featured in the 2019 movie *The Two Popes.* Director Fernando Meirelles features Cardinal Bergoglio carrying his own luggage and taking the bus to the Vatican. In the days after his election as pope, Francis refused the Vatican chauffeur and rode on the bus "with the guys" (i.e., cardinals) to the Sistine Chapel for Mass. When a person of faith makes a conscious choice to share space and time with, to transit with, to engage with their neighbors, the culture sees this not as a publicity stunt but as an act of authentic humility and authentic spirituality! This is validated by the fact that the pope taking public transit is covered by the news media and highlighted in a movie and is the central point of an illustrated children's book.

Risk Widening the Circle

When I started walking, bicycling, and taking public transit, I started meeting new people left and right. One of those people was Michele Molstead, the former director of outreach for Nice Ride, a bike-share program in the Twin Cities. For the Sunday during Bike Week, usually the second week in May, I invited Michele to give a personal reflection about riding a bike as part of her witness for eco-justice. Almost every Sunday, someone from the Judson community gives a five- to ten-minute personal reflection, i.e., the mainline Protestant version of a testimony. My invitation to Michele was not the norm; the protocol was to invite only members of Judson to deliver personal reflections. Thankfully, I didn't know that; I only knew Michele had a story to tell and her story might speak to someone in the congregation.

Her words sparked great conversations after worship, but one conversation in particular caught my ear. My wife, Lori, made a beeline for Michele after the service; she wanted to know what kind of footwear Michele wore while biking. Reader, remember I am not talking about shoes that go with clipless pedals. I'm referring to shoes for professional wear (Lori is a public-school math teacher). Michele recommended Dansko shoes, Danish-inspired, American-designed. This is not a product endorsement, but it illustrates how stories have the capacity to both nudge individuals and initiate risk, to encourage and move people to live anew. All Lori needed to start biking to work was a nudge by someone who looked like her and was not covered head to toe in spandex. When we got home after church, Lori sat down at the dining table and opened up her laptop. I went upstairs to change into post-worship napping attire. When I came downstairs, she had a big grin on her face and she announced, "I'm going to do it!" "Do what?" I asked. "I'm going to start biking to work."

Risk Cooperating with Other Churches: It's Not a Competition

One of the great lessons of walking, biking, and taking public transit for me and Judson Church is to risk cooperation with other people and institutions, to trust strangers, and to forgo the ideas of independence. Judson Church does not have the staff or resources for a full-time social worker to help those in our community with basic needs of food, housing, and medical bills, but Bethlehem Lutheran (a church of note) does, and they are happy to have us partner with their team in this ministry. Judson Church would love to have an outdoor labyrinth, but we do not have space for it. But Bethel Lutheran has one and they are happy to let us use it! Judson Church does not have the resources to fill an entire year with engaging and well-known speakers, but our local churches of note do. During the pandemic we learned to rely on the churches-of-note programming to supplement our educational offerings. COVID-19 forced small city-neighborhood churches to risk interdependence and cooperation. We now have access via Zoom to attend lectures, seminars, and continuing education events we never thought possible before. Judson Church folks can listen to scholars and artists deliver lectures or attend book groups with people from all over the world or sit in silence with strangers in the comfort of their own homes. This model of interdependence reveals how small city-neighborhood churches can stop trying to be omni-churches or the Walmarts of church and be more like boutique shops catering to the needs of their neighbors and neighborhoods.

This model of cooperation has produced a nonpaying side hustle: church brokerage. Because the members of Judson are in relationship with members and programming at other churches, we can help recommend congregations for members of the community. We are not in competition with other churches, so we can risk recommending another church over Judson. Not everyone who finds Judson, or everyone Judson finds, needs to be a member of Judson. Maybe someone likes more formal worship than Judson offers; maybe someone desires more programming; maybe someone wants a more conservative theology. Judson Church does not have to take those needs, wants, and wishes personally and can freely recommend another congregation in the neighborhood or parish that might fit someone's needs better.

Risk Being Late

Yes, I have arrived at meetings late (because the bus was not on time) and sweaty (because I had to pedal quickly to get to my destination). Yes, I have taken the wrong bus and ended up ten miles in the wrong direction. Yes, I have missed a turn on my bike and ended up on a busy road with cars zooming past me at 50 mph. Many times, parishioners (and family members) have called me in a panic, saying, "I'm at the corner of Nicollet and 4th Avenue. Which bus do I take to get to Judson (or back home)?" Or "I'm on the Greenway with a flat tire without a patch kit or a space tube. Can you help me?"

But being late is a risk we'll have to take, because what we lose in punctuality we gain in the shared experience of those we transit with. In her essay "Taking the Train: a Theological Journey through Contemporary Los Angeles County, " Sheila Briggs, University of Southern California Associate Professor of Religion and Gender Studies, reveals how when we take public transit we are sharing space with other passengers and "traveling with them through an urban space in which all of our lives were (are) emplotted."[5] Briggs elaborates that when we transit privately in a car, we lose a sense of solidarity with the masses of humanity who call our cities home. Public transit is one of the few places where this sense of solidarity is restored, even if only for a few minutes. "Thus, taking the train (public transit) has the potential to expand one's social as well as physical vision."[6]

My social and physical vision expanded when I took the bus to a continuing education seminar at Planned Parenthood in St. Paul. As I exited the bus and walked toward the Planned Parenthood facility, I found myself walking through a gauntlet of protesters. They yelled at me, they told me I was going to hell, and they held up graphic images on placards as I approached the front door. Once inside, after going through three locked doors, each time showing ID and getting checked to see if I was on the approved list to enter, I sat down in a chair and thought of all the people throughout the years who sought healthcare as they exited the bus and walked, vulnerable and exposed, to the front doors at Planned Parenthood.

Something mundane could happen on the bus that expands your physical and social vision. One day as Monica, a Judson member, was on the bus, the driver took a sharp right turn that caused a bag of groceries in the front of the bus to overturn. Inside the grocery bag were a dozen oranges. All twelve oranges rolled out of the bag and down the aisle to the back of the bus.

Monica said she and the other passengers were captivated as they watched the oranges slowly roll by. The bus driver, seeing what happened, pulled over to a stop so the passengers could help retrieve the oranges. Once they were picked up and returned to the owner, the passengers smiled at one another and clapped with cheer. In total this may have taken three minutes, but it connected Monica to her other passengers and still provides a reference point for her when seeking compassion and connectivity with strangers. Human beings are social creatures; we desire company; we did not evolve over millions of years to transit alone! We need to share space; we need our senses to be aroused by the communities around us. Those interactions outweigh being late, occasionally, to meetings and gatherings.

You will not always be late. As time goes by and you become more familiar with the transit system, walking routes and bicycle paths, you will adjust, you will arrive on time, and you will not be sweaty. If you are running behind because of your transit choice, call and communicate; most people will understand. I have even found when I do arrive late; people are curious about how the public transit system works. Over time I have found these same curious people will ask to ride the bus with you or will at least ask to pick you up. Again, be patient because what you gain in social experiences will far outweigh the resistance.

Risk Having Messy Conversations

So many times I heard congregants say they wanted to be involved in racial justice but were afraid of saying the wrong thing or doing the wrong thing or offending another person. This fear kept them from acting on issues and causes that they wanted to act on. By nurturing a culture of risk, you can encourage one another to have messy conversations, to not let the fear of making mistakes keep you from action. I constantly remind the congregation, and they constantly remind me, and outside facilitators and consultants and teachers remind us all: Anti-racism work is messy, but don't let the messiness keep you from doing the work.

I define messiness as the difficult inward and outward change that takes place when one moves from the grip of racism to being anti-racist. This change is ever-present and ongoing, therefore messy. Sometimes painful emotions rise to the surface in your relationships, sometimes a breakthrough emerges, sometimes you cannot keep shame at bay, sometimes all you can say is "I'm sorry," sometimes all you feel is love and solidarity and communion; it's messy. Rather than tracing a linear path, this transformation is more spiral-shaped, with plenty of two steps forward, one step back: it's messy.

In 2018, fifty members of Judson went to Memphis, Tennessee, on a three-day racial justice pilgrimage. We visited the National Civil Rights Museum, Slave Haven Underground Railroad Museum, and the Stax Museum of American Soul Music. When we returned to Minneapolis, I asked people to share their experiences as personal reflections, to talk about their messy experiences: the pain, the injustice, the movements of their hearts, what brought tears to their eyes, how they went deep, and the changes they sought to make.

Upon returning from Memphis, Brad told his longtime friends TJ and Richard about his experience. Brad's sharing inspired an idea: The three of them would drive to Memphis together so they could go on their own racial justice pilgrimage. After they returned, I invited the three of them to share their experiences with the Judson community. The four of us chose a Sunday and created a worship service centered on their stories, and then the three friends, one Black and two white, shared their experiences. What struck all of us who heard their stories was how messy they were. Even though they were longtime friends, they had never traveled together; they were worried the trip might cause friction in their friendship; they were worried they might say the wrong thing. But they told us how they leaned into their fears and took the risk. On that Sunday morning as they told their stories about the risks they took with their trip, I could feel the entire congregation move forward. The three men took a risk, and by telling their story, invited us all to take a risk too.

Risk Becoming a Witness

The more you walk, pedal, and take public transit, the more you will begin to pay attention to the neighborhood/community/parish your faith community calls home. The more you are present, the more strangers become neighbors. You start to notice how difficult it must be for an English-language learner to navigate your transit system, or what it is like to be a person who is physically disabled who depends on the bus to get from points A to B. You begin to notice how your city is divided because of socially engineered interstate roads, railroad lines, and industrial sites. You take the time to realize that if our bike lanes were separated from traffic, were safer and easier to ride, kids (and adults) would not ride on the sidewalks. You become aware of joys and struggles you never noticed before.

In the winter of 2018 I included this story in a commentary I wrote for the *Star Tribune*:

"I boarded a bus in Minneapolis and headed south to visit a grieving family. As the bus trundled along it paused to let on an elderly passenger. The passenger boarded gingerly and remarked while paying, 'It's one of those blue-cold days where you say thanks when the bus door opens.' A mile or so later, the elderly passenger pulled the stop cord, and the bus acknowledged it by announcing 'stop requested.' The passenger shuffled to the door and slowly exited. All seemed well until the passenger yelled, 'I'm down, I fell. Please help me.'

"As the passenger pleaded for assistance, the bus driver looked at me and asked if I would be willing to help. I was. As we positioned ourselves on the sidewalk, the passenger asked us to be gentle, mindful of artificial knees. The driver and I wedged our feet underneath the rider's, gripped a hand and an elbow, then lifted with all our might. After becoming vertical, the passenger embraced me in a bear hug and said, 'Do not let go till I get settled.' I held on tight. Once sure footing and equilibrium were established, the passenger thanked us for our help and walked toward home. If I had been driving my car (a Dodge van; I'm not anti-auto), I would not have seen this incident. But if I had been walking by, or riding in the bike lane, I would have (just as I did aboard public transit)."[7]

In response to this commentary, one person replied, "Many of us do not want to feel connected to strangers."[8] I respect the honesty of this comment, even though I disagree with it. Desiring to be disconnected from others is a temptation the biblical writers sought to address. "You shall love your neighbor as yourself" (Leviticus 19:18). I view walking, riding my bike, and taking public transit as a faith practice that places me in touch with people in an intimate manner that I cannot replicate in a car; this practice creates more opportunities for me to love God, creation, my neighbor, and myself. They offer me ways to enter into relationships that will change my life for the better. They are also forms of public and social witness. After I told the above story in a sermon I had a parishioner come up to me and say, "For weeks I have been upset with your stories and I realize why now. You are sharing more time with the poor; you are showing us that we too need to do this."

Dr. Marvin McMickle, former president of Colgate Rochester Crozer Divinity School, in his book *Be My Witness: The Great Commission for Preachers,* defines witness as a threefold method. A witness is someone who sees something, a witness is someone who sees something and says something, and a witness is someone who sees something, says something, and is willing to suffer for something.[9] It is difficult for faith communities to see something, say something, and suffer for something while living protected lives. When we walk, when we bike, and when we take public transit, we see others we've never seen before, we are encouraged to use our place of privilege to say something, and we suffer for and with others we did not know before. I am not asking people of faith to place themselves in harm's way just because. Instead, I am encouraging Christians to challenge the notion of safe, protected, and isolated Christianity by practicing an active witness in their neighborhoods.

When I first proposed McMickle's threefold definition of witness, the congregation was with me for the first two definitions, but the third definition scared some of them—it scared me too. Other members, however, were way ahead of me. One morning several members of the congregation and I attended a training class on civil disobedience for racial justice. During the training, the young black leaders stated they were not going to subject themselves to police brutality for this movement in the Twin Cities. To my astonishment, a white church member of Judson raised his hand and volunteered, "I'm retired. I've got nothing left to prove; an arrest on my record is not a deterrent for me." Another time several church members and I attended a seminar on becoming a sanctuary church to house those who were threatened with deportation by Immigration and Customs Enforcement. The leaders outlined what would be involved for a community of faith to become a sanctuary church. After hearing the proposal, all I could find were reasons not to proceed (plumbing upgrades, space allocation, volunteers, etc.), but to my surprise, the members in attendance ignored my reluctant pragmatism and started investigating for themselves!

Risk Looking Like the
Neighborhood/Community/Parish

The Judson Church profile fits the profile of many mainline liberal small city-neighborhood churches: mostly middle-class and almost exclusively white (98 percent white, 2 percent BIPOC).

Our congregational profile matches neither the profile of the immediate neighborhood (83 percent white, 17 percent BIPOC) nor the current city of Minneapolis profile (63 percent white, 37 percent BIPOC). We are also not well-positioned to match the projected city of Minneapolis profile of 2040, when the city will achieve a majority-minority demographic.

The more we are present in the neighborhood, community, and parish, the more we realize we do not reflect those who call the neighborhood, community, and parish home. Although 70 percent of our membership lives within the three-mile circle/parish, it is a self-selecting 98 percent white congregation. Judson Church feels that the only way toward a sustainable and thriving future is to reflect the neighborhood, community, and parish. Can we take the risk of seeking to change the congregation from 98 percent white and 2 percent BIPOC to mirror the demographic of the neighborhood, 83 percent white and 17 percent BIPOC?

We are starting small, with a land recognition statement and investigation into how Judson Church acquired the land it calls home on the corner of 41st and Harriet. We are using the language skills of our congregation to pray and sing in Spanish. We are intentional about the images of Jesus we use in worship (no more Nordic, fresh-from-the-spa Jesus images). We are intentional about the formation of a BIPOC business directory and our reparations fund. And we are looking for ways to connect and do ministry with the black, Latino, and indigenous churches within the neighborhood, community, and parish. We know this will take time. We know changes will be difficult and messy and we know this will change the church. Our challenge will be whether we can open ourselves up enough, whether we can make ourselves vulnerable enough to allow the neighborhood/community/parish to convert us so that Judson Church mirrors the neighborhood/community/parish.

When Mister Rogers was stressed or anxious, he used to quote a wise saying from one of his teachers: "If it's mentionable, it's manageable." I am not proposing reckless risks but manageable risks, risks that you and your church can do for the sake of creating a more neighborhood-centric, thriving congregation. Now get going!

Prayer, in the Spirit of Howard Thurman

Give us the courage to live! Really live—not merely exist.
Live dangerously.
Embracing risk!
Gracious God, hear our prayer; Give us the courage to live.

Experiment: How to Welcome Risk

Here is an exercise to start welcoming risk. During your next church council or governing body meeting, ask someone from the neighborhood or parish to attend your meeting. Ask them to be a set of neutral ears to listen to the conversations and discussion of the meeting. At the end of the meeting, ask the neighbor to reflect on what they heard and experienced.

- When did you engage in "church talk" or insider language?
- Did anything you discussed in the meeting pertain to the neighborhood or neighbors?
- If this meeting had never taken place, how would the absence of the meeting affect the neighborhood and neighbors?
- What part of the evening caused you to feel energized or challenged?
- Ask the neighbor to note when they detected you were taking a risk.
- Ask the neighbor what risks they would recommend you take, based on the evening's conversation and direction.

Questions for Reflection

1. How many names of the members of your congregation do you know? How many stories of the members do you know? How can you get to know more names and stories?

2. Describe a time when you were encouraged and supported to take a risk in church. What risks do you wish the church encouraged and supported you in?

3. Who in your life has encouraged and supported you to take risks? Who have you encouraged and supported to take risks?

4. List all of the risks in the Bible. If you do not know of any, start a Bible study on just that subject.

5. Make a list of five risks you would like to take this year.

6. In what ways does your church think of itself or operate as a "church of record"?

7. In what ways does your church function as a "church not of record"?

8. Describe how your church could be more like the neighborhood and its immediate neighbors.

9. Make a list of five small goals you and the church governing board of your congregation could take within the next six months.

10. Describe a messy conversation you have recently experienced.

Suggested Reading List

McMickle, Marvin A. *Be My Witness: The Great Commission for Preachers* (Valley Forge, PA: Judson, 2016). A fantastic resource for the role and importance of witnessing.

Pentland, John. *Fishing Tips: How Curiosity Transformed a Community of Faith* (Toronto: United Church, 2019). This book is difficult to obtain in the US. I suggest you order, in bulk, directly from the United Church of Canada (https://ucrdstore.ca/). Also, go to https://hillhurstunited.com to sign up for Hillhurst's email list.

Winter, Emily. *I Got Rejected 101 Times, New York Times* op-ed, December 18, 2018. Also search for videos on YouTube of Winter talking about her year of rejections.

Subscribe to the Rev. Dr. Michael Piazza's daily email, "Liberating Word: Equipping Progressive People of Faith to Be Champions for Peace and Justice" at http://liberatingword.com.

Resources from the Lewis Center for Church Leadership are well worth your time. https://www.churchleadership.com

Recipe: Treat Yourself to Grape Nut Chocolate Chip Cookies

Makes about two dozen (depends on how big you make them)

INGREDIENTS
½ cup softened butter
½ cup firmly packed dark brown sugar
½ cup granulated sugar
2 eggs, room temperature
2 teaspoons vanilla
1 teaspoon baking soda
¼ teaspoon salt
1 tablespoon malt powder
2 cups thick oats
½ cup bread flour
½ cup Grape-Nut flour (place about ¾ cup of Grape-Nuts cereal in a spice mixer and grind for a couple of minutes until it makes a fine flour)
1 cup Grape-Nuts cereal
1 cup chocolate chips
½ cup sunflower seeds (optional)

A Parting Image . . .

Imagine a Sunday morning a year or two or three from today. Because you have encouraged people to walk, bike, and take public transit to church, they may arrive on Sunday morning a little sweaty, and they may not arrive on time. Because of this transit shift, you may find yourself with a congregation outfitted in athleisure wear rather than power suits. Because you have gotten to know the neighborhood and neighbors, there really aren't surprise guests attending; they are friends from previous engagements. After the benediction has been proclaimed, you walk to the plaza (it's not just a parking lot), bend down and pick a straw-

DIRECTIONS
1. Preheat oven to 350 degrees.
2. Beat butter and sugar in a large bowl with an electric mixer or a stand mixer on medium speed until smooth. Add eggs, one at a time, and vanilla; mix well.
3. Add baking soda, salt, malt powder, thick oats, flours, add chocolate chips, sunflower seeds, and Grape-Nuts. Combine until just mixed.
4. With ice cream scoop, drop balls of dough 2 inches apart onto parchment-lined or greased cookie sheets. Lightly flatten the dough balls with the back of a spoon to half-inch thickness. Bake for 10–14 minutes or until golden brown.
5. Cool 2–3 minutes; remove from baking sheets. Cool completely on wire racks. Enjoy.
6. You can store these in an airtight container, but they'll be gone by morning.

berry off the vine (from the straw bale gardening patch), eat it right then, and let the juice dribble down your chin. As you look around, you see some neighborhood youths playing basketball in the corner (because it's for the community, not just for temporary storage of automobiles). They see you and ask, "Play one game with us?" You smile and wave them off but are thankful they asked. You head home, walking or rolling or pedaling or taking public transit, with your heart softened and opened a little more. You are ready to meet others, catch stories, and move the universe one millimeter toward increasing the love of God, love of neighbor, and love of self. Amen.

NOTES

1. Michael Piazza, *Vital Vintage Church: How Traditional Congregations Thrive* (self-published, 2016), 62.
2. Emily Winter, "I Got Rejected 101 Times," nytimes.com, December 14, 2018, https://www.nytimes.com/2018/12/14/opinion/sunday/writers-rejections-resolutions.html.

3. Patrick Madden, "On 'His Last Game,'" Assay: Journal of Non-Fiction Studies, 4.1 Fall 2017, https://www.assayjournal.com/patrick-madden-on-his-last-game.html.

4. Barry Newman, "A-Heds: The Wall Street Journal's Page Column Explained," November 15, 2010, https://www.wsj.com/articles/SB10001424052702303362404575580494180594982.

5. Sheila Briggs, "Taking the Train: A Theological Journey through Contemporary Los Angeles County" in *Spirit in the Cities: Searching for Soul in the Urban Landscape*, ed. by Kathryn Tanner (Minneapolis: Fortress, 2004), 2.

6. Ibid., 5.

7. G. Travis Norvell, "Community Awareness: How Well Can You See from Your Car?" Commentary section, January 11, 2018, in the *Star Tribune*, Minneapolis, MN, http://www.startribune.com/community-awareness-can-you-see-from-your-car/468684513/.

8. Comment by "arspartz", January 13, 2018, 1:54 p.m.

9. Marvin McMickle, *Be My Witness: The Great Commission for Preachers* (Valley Forge, PA: Judson Press, 2016), 62.

But Now You Say . . .

You've heard it said, "You have to choose between church renewal and social justice."

But you say, "Church renewal is social justice and social justice is church renewal. If we are moving in the neighborhood/community/parish, listening, responding with hearts cracked open, social justice and church renewal will happen simultaneously."

You've heard it said, "Small churches will be extinct by 2050."

But you say, "Small churches are vital institutions where everyone knows your story, loves the numbness out of you, and encourages you to take risks for the sake of the gospel."

You've heard it said, "You need parking and parking lots to grow a church."

But you say, "Our parking lot is for more than storing cars for a few hours; it is a plaza for feeding, playing, housing, spiritual growth. And those of us who do not have a parking lot, it is okay, we have more than enough parking when we move in and with our neighborhood/community/parish."

You've heard it said, "Only extroverted leaders can turn around an established church (and even then, the odds are slim)."

But you say, "We can use our greatest human asset: our ears as we conduct one-on-one conversations with our community. We can listen and respond to the needs of our community rather than guessing what they need."

You've heard it said, "You need an established and well-maintained social media presence to reach new people."

But you say, "We love our website and are proud of our Facebook, Instagram, Twitter, YouTube, and even Pinterest pages. But what we are most proud of is knowing our neighbors and the aromas wafting out of their kitchens, knowing the bus drivers' names, handing out biscuits to the dogs when they walk by, and ringing the bells on our bikes as we say hello and goodbye to our neighbors."

You've heard it said, "You need a well-trained, youthful staff to turn around a church."

But you say, "Our 'staff' is like none other. Who would have thought so much talent and energy and wisdom was sitting in our pews all along!"

You've heard it said, "Churches need to rebrand themselves, change their name, and restructure their bylaws."

But you say, "We've all sat in the Fellowship Hall plenty of times contemplating changing our name. And we've all spent hours envisioning a new governance structure, but nothing has ever felt as invigorating, energizing, and meaningful as our walks in the neighborhood, the close connections made, and the new relationships formed since we started listening."

Appendix A
A Prayer for Sidewalks

For the 2017 Christmas Eve service at Judson Church, I invited people from the community to share prayers for the neighborhood. The newly elected councilmember, the retiring state senator, leaders of nonprofits we partner with, students and teachers, and Bill Lindeke, the executive director of streets.mn, all offered prayers. I asked Bill to deliver a prayer for sidewalks.

A Christmas Prayer for Streets and Sidewalks

> *God bless our sidewalks, and the spaces that bring us closer to each other every day. Instill in us the strength to listen, and give our cities, parks, and streets the grace of rich connections.*
>
> *Bless us with the patience to treat each other with kindness, toleration, and love, even when our world makes this a difficult task, even in the thousand rushed hours of our daily routines.*
>
> *Let anger and frustration fall from our thoughts and roll off our backs like raindrops from the awning of a corner store.*
>
> *Let us travel with the relaxing poise of a drifting cloud.*
>
> *God, give us the strength to love our neighbors as ourselves, to shovel the ice and snow from our sidewalks, to trim our hedges, and share the benches in our parks.*
>
> *Give us the wisdom to be stewards of our inheritance, the parks, buildings, trees, and countless nonhuman lives that form the cities where we make our homes.*

Give us the vision to see and know the people that dwell in public places, not just those that speak our language or share our taste in music, but even the strangers to our eyes.

Give us the grace to share our space, our thoughts, and our streets in new ways, to reward ourselves with the compassion, care, and camaraderie that comes from lives of rich connection.

God grant us the beauty of long walks.

Let us understand ourselves as we understand our streets.

Let our perambulations be like pilgrimages along our sidewalks and through our alleys. Give us the patience for a pedestrian pace.

Allow us to breathe freely as we go on our way and grant us the space for serendipity. Let us discover new and precious things even in our own backyards.

Let us hear the sounds of birds, bells, laughter, and the rustling of leaves as we wind our way through the coming new year.

God, thank you for this life we live together and grant us the grace to receive it with curious eyes, open hearts, and springs in our steps.

Amen.

Appendix B
Bicycle Prayer Cards

Each year before school begins, Judson Church hosts a Blessing-palooza: Beasts, Backpacks, and Bikes (we love alliteration). We first held this event inside the sanctuary, but no one wanted to bring their bikes inside and the beasts were always too unruly. So, we moved the event outside onto the sidewalk. One, this created more space for the beasts and owners. Two, it allowed for more members of the neighborhood to participate. We provide a St. Francis charm for the beasts, a prayer card to keep inside your backpack, and a bicycle spoke prayer card. Write a prayer/blessing (see example below), print it out on 3x5 cards, place them in 3x5 laminate pouches, run them through your laminator (most churches have laminating machines) and—voila—instant bespoke bicycle prayer cards. These cards are woven through the spokes of a bicycle wheel.

May your wheels always spin true,
May your brakes always grab,
May drivers always see you, and
May the smile
Only riding a bike can evoke
always remain on your face.
Happy riding.